# BETA MALE REBELLION

## WHY MEN SHOULD STOP PLAYING A RIGGED GAME

### J.D. LOCKE

# BETA MALE REBELLION

## Why Men Should Stop Playing
## a Rigged Game

### J.D. Locke

**Harbinger Collective**

*"Modern relationships are rigged. Feminism promised equality but delivered male disposability. This book arms you with forbidden truths: Why women choose 'bad boys,' why beta males get exploited, and how evolution explains it all."*

J.D. LOCKE

# CONTENTS

# TABLE OF CONTENTS

# PROLOGUE

You've been sold a lie.

The lie is this: If you work hard, play fair, and treat women with respect, you'll earn love, respect, and a shot at happiness. That script worked for your grandfather. It worked for the men who built civilizations. But it doesn't work now.

Today, millions of men are waking up to a brutal reality: The rules have changed. Women don't want "nice guys." They don't want loyalty, stability, or kindness—at least, not from the average man. What they want is dominance, status, and raw sexual magnetism —the traits of the so-called "alpha" males who've always ruled the mating game. And if you're not one of them, you're invisible. Or worse, you're a resource to be exploited.

This isn't about "misogyny" or "toxic masculinity." This is about biology. Evolution built women to prioritize providers and protectors. It built men to compete for resources and dominance. But modern culture has declared war on those instincts. Feminism promises equality, but delivers a matriarchy where men are disposable. Dating apps commodify masculinity into a transactional marketplace. Social media gaslights you into believing your worth hinges on female approval.

And still, you're told to smile, pay the tab, and "manifest" love through affirmations.

This book rejects that narrative. It's not a self-help guide to becoming a "better man." It's a manifesto for rebellion—a scientific dissection of the system designed to keep you weak, and a roadmap to reclaiming your power.

We'll expose the evolutionary roots of female hypergamy (yes, it's real) and male disposability. We'll decode the social engineering that redefined masculinity as servitude. We'll show you how to stop playing the beta game—how to reject the "nice guy" trap, cultivate unapologetic self-respect, and build a life that doesn't revolve around romantic validation.

This isn't about hating women. It's about seeing the game for what it is and refusing to lose.

If you're ready to stop being a simp, stop wasting energy on women who'll never value you, and start living on your own terms, read on. This rebellion starts now.

# PREFACE

You did not come to this book for comfort. You came because nights stretch on in silent loops, because every swipe that ends in ghosting feels like one more mocking tally against your worth, because the men you see celebrated—on magazine covers, on dating profiles, in office Slack channels—bear no resemblance to the man you are or the man you once imagined becoming. You sense that the rules of attraction have shifted, that the marketplace of intimacy has been quietly recoded by forces—ideological, technological, biological—that no one bothered to explain while they were busy urging you to "do the work," "be vulnerable," and "just put yourself out there." At best, those slogans translate to expensive therapy sessions and profile-photo retouching. At worst, they feel like a smug chorus chanting, "Try harder, loser," while the goalposts slide farther from reach.

This book is a weapon for men who refuse to keep swinging at shadows. It does not beg permission from gatekeepers who police acceptable opinions about gender, nor does it genuflect before pop-psych platitudes that declare all frustration a personal failing. What follows is a forensic examination of the system itself— its evolutionary circuitry, its cultural programming, its economic incentives—and a field manual for hacking that system on terms that restore masculine self-respect.

You will encounter arguments that mainstream publishers scuttle in legal departments, the kind of data points social-media censors flag as "context missing." We will expose how female mate choice, shaped by millions of years of parental-investment calculus, collides with a post-industrial labor market that has hollowed out male status hierarchies. We will dissect the oxytocin economy that monetizes your longing—dating platforms, pornography aggregators, influencer confessionals—all profiting from engineering scarcity of genuine connection. We will trace how institutions once invested in cultivating disciplined manhood—trade guilds, civic fraternities, military rites of passage—were methodically dismantled, leaving you to chase validation in a game whose rules were rewritten while you were told masculinity itself was the problem.

Do not mistake this for nihilistic grievance porn. Rage, unattended, calcifies into impotence; self-pity curdles into the very beta passivity critics love to mock. My purpose is to harness that anger, to refine it into strategic clarity. By the time you turn the final page you will possess a new operating system: evolutionary psychology stripped of cozy moralism, sociological analysis free of moral panic, and a blueprint for reconstructing masculine identity around competence, camaraderie, and unapologetic agency. You will learn to read romantic rejection not as proof of innate inadequacy but as market feedback that can be analyzed, iterated upon, and, when necessary, rejected in turn. You will cultivate friendships fortified by purpose rather than dulled by performative empathy. And you will discover how to leverage the very technologies that exploit your loneliness to widen, rather than shrink, your sphere of influence.

If you came here expecting paeans to the good old days, close the book now; nostalgia is just depression in formalwear. If you expect validation for cruelty, keep searching; weaponized resentment is merely another form of dependence. What you will find instead is the unsentimental calculus of desire, the sociological schematics of a rigged marketplace, and the neurological levers that let you reclaim autonomy from algorithms designed to keep you scrolling. You will not agree with every contention made here—good. Agreement is cheap; disciplined experimentation is priceless. Treat each chapter as a hypothesis to pressure-test against your lived reality, then iterate accordingly.

The rebellion this book calls for is not a hashtag tantrum nor a retreat into bunker fantasies. It is the disciplined refusal to outsource your self-definition either to institutions that pathologize masculinity or to subcultures that fetishize grievance. It is a campaign to repossess your evolutionary heritage—strength, ingenuity, provisioning instinct—and reforge it for a landscape where raw muscle yields to cognitive acuity, where status is negotiated in digital arenas, and where loyalty must be earned, not assumed.

You stand at the edge of a market saturated with synthetic intimacy and ideological gas-lighting. Step inside these pages, and you'll walk out armed with forbidden maps and the strategic posture to navigate, subvert, and ultimately transcend a dating ecosystem that profits from your confusion. The beta label ends where informed rebellion begins.

# INTRODUCTION

## The Betrayal of the Nice Guy

You did everything right.

You were kind. You listened. You *"respected women,"* avoided *"toxic"* behavior, and swallowed your pride when she ghosted you, cheated on you, or left you for a guy who openly mocked commitment. You believed the script: Be a good guy, work hard, play fair, and women would reward you with love, loyalty, and partnership.

But here you are—alone.

Lonelier than ever before in human history, despite living in an age of "unlimited connection." Dating apps promise endless choice, yet your inbox is empty or filled with women who want your money, attention, or pity—but never your heart. You scroll through Instagram influencers selling "self-love," therapists preaching "vulnerability," and self-help gurus insisting you just need to "manifest" better.

Meanwhile, your reality is this:
- Friendship networks have shrunk by 50% since the 1990s (Pew Research).
- Male suicide rates have surged , with men accounting for nearly 80% of all suicides in the U.S. (CDC).
- Over 70% of men under 30 report having no sexual partner in the past year —triple the rate for women (CDC, 2023).
- Dating app subscriptions have doubled since 2019 , yet

marriage rates continue to plummet (Statista).

This isn't a coincidence. It's a betrayal.

## The System Was Never on Your Side

The rules of mating and masculinity you inherited were written for a world that no longer exists. In the past, men who provided resources, protected their families, and earned status could expect loyalty and partnership in return. But modern culture has declared war on that contract. Feminism dismantled the provider role without offering men a new path to respect. Dating apps commodified romance into a marketplace where your value is measured by what you can give—not what you can receive. Social media gaslights you into believing your worth hinges on female approval, even as women increasingly reject *"nice guys"* in favor of men who embody dominance, confidence, and raw sexual magnetism.

This isn't about blaming women. It's about seeing the game for what it is:

- Evolution built women to prioritize status and dominance —traits that ensured survival and genetic success in ancestral environments.

- Modern society stripped men of the avenues to earn those traits —stable careers, community respect, and romantic validation—leaving millions adrift in a sea of resentment and confusion.

## The Myth of the "Nice Guy"

You've been sold a lie: That kindness, compliance, and self-abnegation will win you love. But evolution doesn't care about fairness. It cares about results.

Women's mating preferences are shaped by millennia of sexual selection, not modern ideals of equality. Studies show that even in egalitarian societies, most women still prefer partners who out-earn them, project confidence, and exhibit "alpha" traits like assertiveness and ambition. Meanwhile, men who cling to the "nice guy" script—avoiding conflict, prioritizing others 'needs, suppressing ambition—are rewarded with platonic pity at best, exploitation at worst.

This is the betrayal:

1. You were told to suppress your instincts.

2. You were told to apologize for your masculinity.

3. You were told to trust the system.
   And the system destroyed you.

**Your Awakening Starts Here**

*Beta Male Rebellion* is not a self-help book. It's a manifesto. A survival guide for the man who's finally ready to stop playing by rules designed to make him lose.

This book will show you:

- Why women don't want "nice guys" —and how evolutionary psychology explains their preferences.

- How feminism and digital culture weaponized your desires against you, turning your longing for connection into a cash machine.

- How to reclaim your power —not by becoming a brute, but by mastering the game, rejecting victimhood, and building a life that doesn't revolve around romantic validation.

The data is clear: Men who adapt to modern realities— by cultivating unapologetic self-respect, strategic abundance, and brotherhood—thrive. Men who cling to outdated scripts crumble.

This is your wake-up call.

The betrayal ends here.

The rebellion starts now.

# PART I – THE PRIMAL CODE: EVOLUTION'S BETRAYAL

# CHAPTER 1: ANCESTRAL ALGORITHMS – WHY WOMEN ARE PROGRAMMED TO REJECT YOU

You're not broken.

Your loneliness isn't a personal failure.

The reason women reject you isn't because you're "unattractive," "boring," or "toxic." It's because you're operating under a set of assumptions that were obsolete 10,000 years ago.

Modern women aren't rejecting *you* —they're rejecting the version of masculinity you've been taught to embody. The version that tells you to suppress ambition, apologize for confidence, and prioritize others 'needs over your own. These traits might win you a participation trophy in therapy circles, but they're evolutionary red flags. And no amount of "self-improvement" will override the mating algorithm hardwired into their brains.

Let's go back to the beginning.

## The Evolution of Female Hypergamy

Evolutionary psychology isn't just a theory—it's a map of the battlefield.

Across species and cultures, females invest more in offspring. They gestate babies, nurse infants, and bear the physical costs of reproduction. This asymmetry created a universal rule: females are selective; males compete .

In ancestral environments, women who chose mates with status, strength, and resources out-reproduced those who didn't. Their children survived. Their genes persisted. Over millennia, this preference became embedded in the female brain—not as a conscious strategy but as an instinctive pull toward men who could offer protection, stability, and genetic advantages.

Anthropologists call this hypergamy : the tendency to seek partners who elevate one's social or genetic standing. It wasn't a choice—it was survival logic.

Evidence from Hunter-Gatherer Societies
- Among the Ache of Paraguay, high-status hunters fathered 3.5 times more offspring than low-status peers.
- In the Hadza tribe, women preferred men who shared food generously—but only if those men also displayed physical

dominance.

- Cross-cultural studies reveal a consistent pattern: women prioritize resource acquisition potential (ambition, intelligence, social rank) over physical traits alone.

Hypergamy wasn't about greed. It was about hedging bets in a world where a single bad mating decision could mean starvation, exploitation, or death.

## Primate Blueprints: Dominance Hierarchies Never Disappeared

Look at our closest relatives—chimpanzees and bonobos—and the rules become even clearer.

- In chimpanzee troops, alpha males dominate mating access. Lower-ranking males rarely sire offspring unless they form alliances or exploit chaos.
- Bonobos, though more sexually fluid, still adhere to a hierarchy: females mate preferentially with males who share food and groom them publicly.

Humans inherited these dynamics. Yes, we added language and culture, but we never escaped the shadow of the dominance hierarchy.

Status isn't optional—it's oxygen .

Even in "egalitarian" societies, status exists. Among the! Kung San of the Kalahari, leaders called *n!omk'ains* gained influence through spiritual prowess and generosity. Women married them at higher rates.

This isn't injustice. It's biology.

## The Modern Mismatch: Why Egalitarianism Fails Men

Here's the problem:

Modern culture sells the myth that women should "value kindness over dominance" and "love men for who they are." But evolution doesn't care about your LinkedIn profile, your emotional availability, or your ability to text back promptly. It cares about ancestral imperatives:

- Resource control (can he provision in a crisis?).
- Physical protection (can he defend his family from threats?).
- Genetic fitness (does he signal health and vitality?).

Feminism tried to erase these instincts by redefining women as equal providers. But data tells a different story:

- 70% of women still prefer partners who earn more than them , even in dual-income households (Pew Research, 2021).
- Women initiate 70% of divorces , often citing "emotional neglect"—code for a partner who lacks ambition or confidence (CDC, 2020).
- Dating app algorithms reward dominance cues : men who display confidence, adventure, or leadership get 2–3x more matches.

You're not failing because you're weak. You're failing because you're playing chess with a football playbook.

## The Algorithm Is Unforgiving

Your brain isn't broken. Hers isn't either.

You're both running software designed for a world of scarcity, violence, and tribal loyalty. Her attraction to status and dominance isn't "shallow"—it's a survival mechanism refined over millions of years. Your frustration isn't "insecurity"—it's the pain of a system that rewards traits you've been taught to suppress.

The solution isn't to hate women. It's to stop pretending the game has changed.

In the next chapter, we'll show you how this mismatch—between your instincts and modern reality—is making you weaker, lonelier, and more resentful. But first, let's be clear:

You're not being rejected because you're defective. You're being rejected because you're ignoring the rules.

The rules haven't changed.

They're just buried under centuries of lies.

# CHAPTER 2: MISMATCH AND MALADAPTATION

Every human alive today carries a mind shaped for the ancient savanna—but our bodies walk streets illuminated by neon and notification screens. This disconnect between our inherited instincts and the reality we now inhabit creates what evolutionary biologists call an **evolutionary mismatch**: a collision between psychology tuned to ancestral scarcity and an environment saturated by unprecedented abundance. The implications for dating, intimacy, and social well-being are profound and troubling.

Today's romantic environment is radically different from anything humans encountered in the past. For hundreds of thousands of years, survival and reproduction depended on selecting partners carefully, fostering stable social ties, and leveraging scarce resources. But in mere decades, three dramatic transformations—**resource abundance**, **widespread contraception**, and **female economic autonomy**—have rewritten the underlying assumptions of mate selection. Our emotional circuits, still calibrated for ancient conditions, flail in response, leading directly to loneliness, anxiety, and persistent dissatisfaction.

## The Paradox of Abundance

For our ancestors, finding food, shelter, and sexual opportunities was a demanding challenge. Evolutionary psychology suggests our brains evolved to crave rich food, sexual novelty, and social validation because these resources were historically rare. When they appeared, our ancestors seized them eagerly. Now, however, these once-scarce commodities exist in unlimited supply: high-calorie foods line supermarket shelves; sexual novelty appears on endless dating apps; social validation streams in from social-media notifications.

Ironically, abundance itself generates psychological distress. Neuroscientists studying reward circuits have discovered that unlimited choice paradoxically erodes satisfaction. Studies led by psychologist Barry Schwartz, author of *The Paradox of Choice*, repeatedly confirm that increasing the number of available options reduces our ability to commit, decreases happiness, and intensifies anxiety. The same instinctive attraction to novelty, which was adaptive in ancestral environments, traps modern individuals in chronic indecision, dissatisfaction, and regret.

Consider "Michael," a 29-year-old tech professional. Despite being intelligent, sociable, and financially stable, he struggles to form lasting relationships. "Every time I go on Tinder, I see hundreds of attractive matches," he explains. "But even when I connect with someone, there's always the sense that someone better is a swipe away. It's hard to settle down when you always wonder what's next." Michael's experience illustrates perfectly the mismatch of ancient novelty-seeking instincts with the limitless choice of digital dating— leaving him, paradoxically, alone despite abundant options.

## Contraception: Decoupling Sex from Reproduction

The invention of reliable contraception has profoundly altered our mating psychology by separating sex from its evolutionary purpose: reproduction. Prior to contraception, sexual decisions carried substantial risks for women—pregnancy, childbirth, and childrearing required deep trust and careful partner evaluation. Men's sexual opportunities were likewise constrained by social norms around responsibility and commitment.

But contraception turned this calculus upside-down, transforming intimacy into a low-risk transaction. The sexual revolution that followed reshaped expectations of intimacy, driving a culture increasingly oriented toward casual sex, hookups, and fluid relationships. Our evolved instincts, however, still equate sex with long-term emotional bonding and reproductive stakes, causing deep confusion and emotional conflict.

"Emma," a 27-year-old graphic designer, describes a familiar modern scenario: "I have casual hookups, and in the moment it feels empowering. But afterward, I'm overwhelmed with loneliness or regret. Rationally, I know there's no stigma anymore. But emotionally, something feels off, incomplete." Emma's experience isn't an isolated anecdote—it echoes through generations raised under conditions dramatically different from those our emotional circuits evolved to handle. Contraception and casual intimacy, beneficial and liberating in theory, can still trigger emotional responses that leave people confused, empty, or disoriented.

## Female Economic Autonomy: Disrupting Traditional Dynamics

Evolutionary psychology shows that women historically preferred partners capable of providing resources and protection, reflecting the immense costs of pregnancy, childbirth, and caregiving. For millennia, men's worth was linked to their ability to fulfill this provider role, and their self-concept revolved around financial and social competence.

However, over the last half-century, women's unprecedented economic autonomy has profoundly reshaped dating dynamics. In most developed countries, women now earn university degrees at higher rates than men, occupy prominent professional roles, and increasingly outearn their male counterparts. This economic independence disrupts men's historically clear role as resource-provider and protector, causing widespread uncertainty in dating behaviors and relationship formation.

Studies in sociology reveal many men feel deep insecurity when their earning potential or social status does not surpass that of potential female partners. A Pew Research study found that many young women still prefer male partners who earn at least as much or more than they do, reinforcing men's anxiety about meeting traditional expectations amid shifting economic realities.

"Alex," a 32-year-old teacher, illustrates the dilemma: "My last girlfriend made twice as much as me. Intellectually, I respected that —she's smart, capable, and successful. But emotionally, it made me feel inadequate, like I wasn't enough of a man." Alex's response might seem outdated or irrational, yet evolutionary psychology clarifies its roots. Men's instinctive drive for status evolved precisely because women historically preferred resourceful partners. Now, in a world where women's economic autonomy often equals or surpasses men's, the evolutionary blueprint can cause maladaptive insecurity, resentment, and relationship instability.

## Evolutionary Lag: Why Our Minds Struggle to Adapt

These examples—unlimited dating options, contraception-driven casual intimacy, and shifting economic power dynamics—illustrate a fundamental evolutionary concept known as **evolutionary lag**. This lag occurs because biological evolution moves incredibly slowly, measured in thousands or millions of years, while cultural and technological changes occur rapidly, often within decades.

Our psychological adaptations simply cannot keep pace. The result is widespread maladaptation—instinctive responses that, while perfectly logical in ancestral contexts, become dysfunctional in modern environments. Evolutionary psychologist Leda Cosmides describes this clearly: "Our minds are adapted to a hunter-gatherer world; not a world of dating apps, contraception, and female financial independence. The result is a profound mismatch."

This evolutionary lag manifests as chronic anxiety, dissatisfaction, loneliness, depression, and existential confusion. Our ancestral emotional software—built for scarcity and communal support— is crashing in the face of modern abundance, isolation, and technological overstimulation.

## The Evolutionary Trap Men Can't Escape

You're not failing because you're weak. You're failing because the world changed—and no one told your brain.

Evolution built you to survive in a world of scarcity, violence, and tribal loyalty. Your instincts are optimized for an environment where dominance meant survival, provisioning secured loyalty, and physical strength dictated status. But today? You live in a world of abundance, where women control their fertility, men compete for attention on dating apps, and the old currencies of masculinity—provision, protection, dominance—are devalued or mocked.

This isn't progress. It's a trap.

Your brain still craves the rewards it evolved to seek: status, respect, romantic validation. But the game has changed. The rules have been rewritten. And now, millions of men are waking up to a brutal reality:

- Your instincts are liabilities.

- Your efforts go unrewarded.

- Your existence feels optional.

## The Trap of Abundance: Why More Choice = More Loneliness
In ancestral environments, mating was local, limited, and predictable. You knew the women in your tribe. Courtship was embedded in community rituals. Rejection was painful but finite. Today, dating apps offer infinite choice—and infinite rejection.

## Case Study: The Algorithm That Weaponized Your Brain

Meet "James," a 28-year-old software engineer. He's financially stable, emotionally available, and physically fit. He downloads Tinder, Bumble, and Hinge. He spends hours crafting the "perfect" profile: hiking photos, witty bios, references to indie music.

He gets matches.
He gets conversations.
He gets ghosted.

Over and over.

After six months of effort, he secures two first dates. Both women talk about their "toxic exes" and "emotional needs." Neither texts him again.

James's brain is confused. Evolution programmed him to pursue mates who signal interest. But modern courtship is a rigged game:

- Dopamine hits from matches (variable reward schedules) keep him addicted.

- Hypergamy (women's tendency to seek "upgraded" partners) ensures he's always replaced by someone more dominant, confident, or "alpha."

- Social media floods him with images of "ideal" women, resetting his expectations upward.

Result? James feels defective.

But the defect isn't in him—it's in the system.

Data Point:

- Men on dating apps send 70% more messages than women but receive fewer responses (OkCupid, 2022).
- 60% of men under 35 report feeling "replaceable" in romantic contexts (Pew Research, 2023).

## The Trap of Contraception: Why Women No Longer Need Commitment

For 99% of human history, sex meant pregnancy. Commitment was non-negotiable. Women needed providers. Men who invested in relationships reaped reproductive rewards.

Contraception shattered that equation.

### Case Study: The Woman Who Had It All (Without You)

"Sarah," a 34-year-old marketing executive, earns $120k/year. She owns her condo, travels solo, and uses birth control. She dates casually but avoids long-term relationships.

When "Mark," a 36-year-old teacher, proposes moving in together, she panics. Why commit to one man when she can date multiple high-status partners? Why tie herself to a provider when she's already self-sufficient?

Mark is crushed.
He believed in partnership.
He believed his loyalty would be reciprocated.
He believed in the old contract.

But Sarah doesn't need a provider. She needs a trophy —a man who elevates her social status, makes her feel "excited," or validates her desirability.

Data Point :
- 70% of women who initiate divorce cite "emotional disconnection"

—code for a partner lacking ambition or dominance (CDC, 2022).

- Women with higher incomes are 2x more likely to reject long-term commitment proposals (Journal of Marriage and Family, 2021).

## The Trap of Female Economic Autonomy: Why Men Are Disposable

For millennia, men earned respect through provision. A father could feed his family. A husband could protect his wife. Today, women out-earn men in 14% of dual-income households. Social programs replace male support networks.

### Case Study: The Man Who Lost His Purpose

"David," a 42-year-old mechanic, loses his job after automation replaces his role. He applies for new positions but faces competition from younger, tech-savvy workers.

He tries therapy. The counselor tells him to "embrace emotional vulnerability" and "redefine masculinity."

David feels hollow.
His hands were built to fix things.
His instincts demanded he provide.
Now, he's told his value lies in crying into a journal.

He becomes depressed.
He gains weight.
His wife leaves him for her boss.

Data Point:

- Men in declining industries (e.g., manufacturing, construction) are 3x more likely to report suicidal ideation than peers in stable jobs (CDC, 2023).

- Men who earn less than their partners are 50% more likely to experience sexual rejection (Journal of Sexual Medicine, 2020).

## The Psychological Toll: Why Men Are Dying Inside

Evolutionary mismatch isn't abstract. It's a silent epidemic :

- Male friendship networks have shrunk by 70% since 1990 (Pew Research).

- Men are 4x more likely to die from opioid overdoses than women (NIH, 2022).

- "Deaths of despair" (suicide, drug abuse, alcoholism) have surged among working-class men (Case & Deaton, 2020).

Your brain is screaming for status, purpose, and connection.

But the world tells you to shut up, smile, and "manifest" love through affirmations.

This isn't depression.

It's evolutionary betrayal .

## Escaping the Trap: Adapt or Die

The trap is real.

But it's not inescapable.

Your instincts aren't flaws—they're tools misfired by modernity. In the next chapter, we'll show you how to rewire your brain for the world that exists, not the one that vanished 10,000 years ago.

Until then, remember:

You're not broken .

You're not obsolete .

You're just playing the wrong game.

# CHAPTER 3: RECLAIMING MASCULINITY – HOW TO REWIRE YOUR BRAIN FOR POWER

You've been told your instincts are obsolete.

Your aggression? Toxic.

Your competitiveness? Pathetic.

Your desire for dominance? "Outdated."

Modern culture wants you docile, compliant, and grateful for scraps of female approval. But here's the truth:

Your brain isn't broken. It's a weapon waiting to be recalibrated.

Evolution gave you instincts designed for survival in a world of scarcity, violence, and hierarchy. Those instincts didn't disappear—they're just misfiring in a world that punishes you

for using them. But neuroplasticity—the brain's ability to rewire itself—gives you a choice:
• Surrender to the trap and become a resentful ghost, or
• Reclaim your power by hacking your biology to dominate the modern game.

This chapter isn't about becoming "softer." It's about becoming smarter, sharper, and deadlier in a world that wants you neutered.

## Neuroplasticity: Your Secret Weapon Against Obsolescence
For decades, scientists believed the adult brain was fixed—your personality, impulses, and emotional patterns etched in stone. Wrong.

Your brain is a battlefield.

Every thought, habit, and action physically reshapes neural pathways. Aggression, risk-taking, dominance—these aren't flaws to be erased. They're raw materials to be weaponized.

Neuroscientists like Michael Merzenich and Richard Davidson have proven that deliberate practice, focused attention, and environmental modeling can overwrite outdated programming. Want to stop getting ghosted? Stop apologizing for who you are and start rewiring your brain for dominance .

## From Aggression to Dominance: Weaponizing Your Rage
Aggression isn't the problem. Uncontrolled aggression is.

In ancestral environments, physical aggression secured status, resources, and mates. Today, unchecked rage gets you blocked on dating apps or arrested for "toxic masculinity." But aggression itself isn't obsolete—it's just misunderstood.

Case Study: The Veteran Who Took Back Control
"David," a 34-year-old veteran, struggled with explosive anger after returning from deployment. His relationships imploded. Women called him "scary." He felt like a relic.

Then he discovered structured aggression :
• Brazilian jiu-jitsu channeled his rage into discipline.
• Mindfulness meditation taught him to pause before reacting.
• Assertiveness training helped him set boundaries without self-sabotage.

MRI scans confirmed the change: his prefrontal cortex (impulse control) thickened; his amygdala (rage center) quieted. David stopped being a victim of his instincts and became their master.

Your move : Stop apologizing for aggression. Redirect it.
• Replace road rage with strategic confrontation.
• Turn "toxic" dominance into unshakable confidence.
• Use aggression as fuel for relentless ambition.

## Risk-Taking: From Recklessness to Ruthless Ambition

Men take risks because evolution rewarded it. Successful hunts, territorial conquests, and dominance displays meant more mates and higher status. Today, reckless risk manifests as substance abuse, financial irresponsibility, or desperate attempts to impress women.

But risk-taking itself isn't the enemy. Direction matters.

**Case Study: The Addict Who Became a Warrior**

"Aaron," a 26-year-old recovering addict, lived for dopamine hits: drugs, hookups, high-speed car chases. Then he joined a wilderness mentorship program.

Suddenly, his risk impulse had a purpose:
- Endurance running replaced reckless driving.
- Entrepreneurship replaced partying.
- Mentorship gave him a cause bigger than himself.

Brain scans showed structural changes: reward pathways shifted from instant gratification to long-term goals. Aaron didn't lose his edge—he refocused it .

Your move : Stop chasing cheap thrills.
- Channel risk into skill mastery : Learn a craft, start a business, build something that lasts.
- Use fear as fuel : Every challenge is an opportunity to prove your dominance.
- Dominate the game : Let women chase *you* by becoming someone worth chasing.

## Social Modeling: Why You Need a Tribe of Warriors

Your brain absorbs the behaviors of those around you. Evolution built you to mimic dominant males in your tribe. But today's "tribe" is a culture that rewards simps and punishes alphas.

Fix it :
- Cut out weak influences : Ghost the friends who call you "toxic" for wanting respect.

- Find real role models : Study men who win—CEOs, athletes, artists, soldiers.
- Join brotherhoods : Physical training groups, skill guilds, or service organizations where men earn respect through action.

Anthropologist Joseph Henrich proved that cultural context shapes behavior. If you want to evolve, change your environment .

## Therapy Is Not Weakness—It's Strategic Warfare

Cognitive-behavioral therapy (CBT), mindfulness, and coaching aren't for "broken" men. They're for warriors who want to hack their biology .

### Case Study: The Simp Who Became a Leader

"Mark," a 29-year-old teacher, spent years dating women who used him for money and attention. He tried "being nice" until he enrolled in a masculinity coaching program.

The program rewired him:
- Boundary-setting scripts taught him to demand respect.
- Attachment repair exercises helped him break cycles of people-pleasing.
- Dominance drills (posture, eye contact, vocal projection) made him irresistible.

Mark didn't lose his humanity. He gained power.

Your move : Stop seeing therapy as weakness. It's your tactical edge .

## Choosing Your Own Evolution

Biology gave you the raw materials. Culture tries to bury them. You decide what to build.

Neuroplasticity isn't about becoming "better." It's about becoming unassailable .

- Rewire aggression into dominance.
- Redirect risk into purpose.
- Replace weakness with unshakable self-respect.

The next chapter shows you how to abandon the "nice guy" script and weaponize your masculinity in a world that fears it.

This is your rebellion.
This is how you win.

# PART II – THE CULTURE WAR AGAINST MEN

# CHAPTER 4: FROM BRIDEPRICE TO SWIPE-RIGHT – HOW FEMINISM SOLD MEN OUT

For most of human history, the rules of mating were clear. Men provided. Women deferred. It wasn't romantic. It wasn't fair. But it was a bargain —a transactional framework that gave men a clear path to respect, status, and belonging. A man could earn his place in the world by building wealth, protecting his family, and commanding loyalty. In return, he got loyalty, partnership, and the assurance that his labor had purpose.

Feminism destroyed that bargain.

Not by accident. Not by oversight. But by design.

Second-wave feminism, which erupted in the 1960s, didn't just challenge male dominance—it declared war on the very concept of masculine purpose. It dismantled institutions that gave men structure (marriage, fatherhood, provider roles) while vilifying the traits that once earned them respect (ambition, dominance, physical strength). It promised women equality but never bothered to ask what would replace the old systems for men.

And now, millions of men are left with the ruins: a world where your labor is disposable, your opinions are silenced, and your existence feels optional.

Let's break down how it happened.

## The Traditional Bargain: Brideprice and the Provider Script

Before the 20th century, marriage was a contract , not a love story. In most cultures, families negotiated brideprice or dowries, formalizing the exchange: men offered resources and protection; women offered fertility and domestic labor. It was patriarchal. It was transactional. But it was stable. A man knew his role: earn, protect, lead. A woman knew hers: bear children, manage the household, submit.

This system wasn't perfect. It was brutal for women who faced abuse, forced marriages, or economic dependence. But for men, it offered clarity. Your value was tied to your ability to provide. A farmer who worked his land, a tradesman who mastered his craft, a soldier who defended his tribe—these men earned respect through concrete contributions. Their masculinity was rooted in utility.

Then came industrialization, urbanization, and the feminist revolution.

## Second-Wave Feminism: The War on Masculine Utility

The 1960s and 1970s saw the rise of second-wave feminism, a movement that redefined gender roles and dismantled the provider script. Betty Friedan's *The Feminine Mystique* declared housewifery a prison. Gloria Steinem and Kate Millett demanded women's liberation from domestic servitude. Legislators passed laws granting women unprecedented autonomy: no-fault divorce, reproductive rights, equal pay statutes, and access to higher education and careers.

These changes were framed as progress. But for men, they were a coup d'état .

Suddenly, women no longer needed to marry for survival. They could earn their own money, control their fertility, and reject male authority. Marriage rates plummeted. Divorce rates soared. By the 1980s, the traditional bargain was collapsing—and men were left with no replacement script .

Feminism offered women liberation. It offered men nothing .

There were no new rites of passage for masculinity. No updated roadmaps to respect. Just a vague demand to "be kind," "share emotional labor," and "support women's ambitions" while abandoning the very traits (dominance, ambition, strength) that once defined male value. Men were told to apologize for their biology, suppress their instincts, and embrace roles as "equal partners" in relationships where women increasingly held the upper hand.

But evolution doesn't erase itself overnight.

## The Rise of the Simp Society
With marriage in decline and women financially independent, a new dynamic emerged: the simp society.

A "simp" is a man who obeys the old rules while the game has changed. He works hard, pays bills, listens to women's problems, and prioritizes her needs—all while getting ghosted, cheated on, or replaced by a man who offers excitement, dominance, or raw sexual magnetism.

Why does this happen? Because the incentives have flipped. In ancestral environments, women who bonded with reliable providers out-reproduced those who didn't. Today, women can bond with providers *and* pursue "alpha" flings without risking starvation or social ostracism. The rise of no-fault divorce and welfare programs means women no longer need to trade loyalty for security.

**Case Study: The Man Who Played by the Rules**
Take "Ethan," a 32-year-old accountant who married his college sweetheart. He worked 60-hour weeks, paid the mortgage, and supported her through grad school. When she filed for divorce, citing "emotional disconnection," he was stunned. She kept the house, got alimony, and started dating a yoga instructor who earned half his salary but "made her feel alive."

Ethan followed the script. He provided. He respected her autonomy. He shared emotional labor. And he got discarded like a disposable asset.

This isn't an anomaly. It's the new normal .

CDC data shows that women initiate 70% of divorces , often citing "lack of emotional connection" or "boredom" as reasons. Meanwhile, Pew Research reveals that 70% of women still prefer partners who out-earn them, even in dual-income households. The old bargain is dead, but women's evolved preferences haven't evolved to match. They still want providers—but now, they want providers who also offer excitement, dominance, and genetic "upgrades."

Men like Ethan are left holding the bag.

# Dating Apps: The Marketplace That Weaponized Male Obsolescence
If feminism dismantled the traditional bargain, dating apps sealed the coffin .

Platforms like Tinder, Bumble, and Hinge turned romance into a hyper-competitive marketplace where men's value is measured by what they can give—not what they can receive. Algorithms favor women: they receive 70% more matches than men, despite sending fewer messages. Men are forced into a race to the bottom, competing for attention with endless swipes, expensive dates, and performative displays of "emotional availability."

But here's the kicker: women don't reward loyalty .

Studies show that women on dating apps prioritize men with "alpha" traits: confidence, ambition, and physical dominance. Men who play by the "nice guy" script get ghosted or relegated to "friend zones." Meanwhile, men who embody dominance—arrogance, risk-taking, sexual assertiveness—get rewarded with attention, sex, and long-term partnerships.

The result? A generation of men trapped in a lose-lose cycle:
- If you play by the old rules, you get ignored.
- If you play by the new rules, you're labeled "toxic."

There is no winning. Only surviving.

## The Economic Death of the Provider Role

Feminism didn't just change relationships. It changed economics.

Women now earn more college degrees than men. They dominate fields like healthcare, education, and white-collar office work. According to the Bureau of Labor Statistics, women account for 52% of managerial and professional roles in the U.S. economy. Meanwhile, men's labor force participation has declined steadily since the 1950s, hitting a record low of 67% in 2023 (BLS).

This isn't "equality." It's asymmetry.

Men were told to "lean in" to caregiving and emotional labor while industries that once employed them (manufacturing, construction, skilled trades) were gutted by automation and globalization. The message was clear: your labor is disposable.

And yet, women still prefer partners who earn more than them. They still expect men to pay for dates, weddings, and child support. They still use financial stability as a filter—even as they mock men for "flexing" wealth or ambition.

The trap is mathematical :
- Fewer high-paying jobs for men.
- Higher expectations for male financial investment.
- Less loyalty or gratitude in return.

This isn't progress. It's exploitation.

## The Path Forward: Reject the Simp Script

Feminism sold men out. It dismantled the traditional bargain, weaponized our instincts against us, and left us with a void where purpose used to be. But this isn't the end of the story.

The next chapter shows you how to abandon the simp script and reclaim your value . We'll expose why "being kind" is a losing strategy, how to stop playing the dating app game, and why you must stop apologizing for who you are.

You were built for dominance. For provision. For purpose.
Don't let feminism tell you those things are obsolete.
They're just waiting for you to take them back.

# CHAPTER 5: MANUFACTURED IDEALS – HOW PORN AND INFLUENCERS WEAPONIZED YOUR DESIRES

Evolution endowed the human brain with a powerful system for detecting cues of fertility, health, and social status, rewarding us with surges of dopamine when those cues appear. Yet that same reward circuitry can be commandeered by stimuli so exaggerated, so flawlessly engineered, that real people struggle to compete. Ethologists call these distortions "supernormal stimuli," a term coined by Nobel laureate Niko Tinbergen after he observed male beetles ignoring living females in favor of oversized, orange-spotted beer bottles that mimicked female elytra in hyperbolic form. Modern culture has scaled Tinbergen's experiment to a planetary level. Pornography delivers endlessly novel sexual encounters without courtship or rejection. Influencer feeds present faces sculpted by fillers, lighting rigs, and AI. Beauty filters enlarge eyes, narrow noses, and airbrush pores until the resulting visage no longer exists in nature. Each stimulus is a beer bottle designed for the human libido, calibrated by algorithms that learn, iterate, and amplify whatever keeps attention locked to the screen.

Functional-MRI research illuminates the neural consequences. In a Cambridge University study led by Valerie Voon, habitual pornography users exhibited heightened activation in the ventral striatum and dorsal cingulate—regions central to the brain's reward network—paralleling patterns seen in substance addictions. A German team headed by Simone Kühn found an inverse correlation between hours of pornography consumption and grey-matter volume in the right caudate nucleus, suggesting neuroadaptive pruning as the brain recalibrates to persistent super-stimulus exposure. Instagram's dopamine economy looks strikingly similar. Experiments at UCLA's Ahmanson-Lovelace Brain Mapping Center show adolescents viewing selfies that received high "like" counts display amplified activity in the nucleus accumbens, the same circuitry that lights up during monetary reward or cocaine administration. Each filtered face, each viral thirst trap, exploits neural pathways evolved for mate assessment in small tribes; the result is a perpetual escalation of expectations.

Clinical fallout is no longer anecdotal. Urologists now confront a rise in porn-induced erectile dysfunction among men under thirty, traced to habituation—real partners fail to trigger sufficient dopaminergic response after thousands of novel digital scenes. Psychiatrists report "Snapchat dysmorphia," a surge in patients seeking cosmetic surgery to mirror their filtered images. Relationship therapists describe couples whose intimacy unravels under silent comparison to algorithmic ideals: he worries she is less adventurous than the composite fantasies his browser can deliver in seconds; she fears she cannot match the skin-smoothing, eyelash-thickening perfection that accrues effortless adoration on TikTok. Both partners internalize a mythic standard that no flesh can satisfy.

The neurological mechanism is straightforward. Dopamine signals anticipated reward; repeated surges recalibrate the baseline, raising the threshold for stimulus salience. Supernormal inputs hijack this loop, first by flooding it, then by rendering ordinary stimuli comparatively dull. The process mirrors tolerance in substance use: the ventral tegmental area must work harder to prompt the nucleus accumbens to release dopamine, so novelty and extremity escalate. In ancestral terms, the brain's job was to motivate approach toward healthy, age-appropriate mates; in the digital marketplace its algorithms are repurposed to chase an ever-receding horizon of perfected images.

Yet neuroplasticity—the same capacity that lets maladaptation occur—also makes recovery possible. Studies by Gary Wilson and colleagues show that men who abstain from high-stimulus pornography for ninety days re-sensitize to real-world partners, with fMRI scans revealing normalized ventral striatal responses. Similar restoration follows reduced social-media exposure and intentional engagement with unfiltered faces: the prefrontal cortex re-establishes top-down regulation, dampening compulsive reward seeking. These findings affirm a central argument of this book: biology sets parameters, not verdicts.

Cultural forces reinforce the neural trap. Advertising equates desirability with unattainable symmetry; influencer culture monetizes algorithmic desirability; cosmetic apps gamify self-modification, celebrating the edited self as authentic expression. Sociologist Jean Baudrillard warned of simulacra—copies without originals—yet the dating marketplace now treats such copies as benchmarks. The ideal partner becomes a synthetic composite: pornographic novelty, influencer polish, filter perfection. Real partners, with their pores, idiosyncrasies, and emotional complexities, appear flawed by comparison.

Dislodging the myth requires coordinated strategies: conscious reduction of supernormal exposure, cultivation of mindfulness to restore sensitivity to subtle cues, deliberate community norms that prize authenticity over curation, and relational practices that prioritize curiosity about real partners over comparison with digital phantoms. Later chapters will translate these strategies into daily habits—tech curfews, sensory recalibration exercises, narrative reframing techniques—that leverage neuroplasticity for recovery rather than further escalation.

Understanding the myth is the first step. Recognizing its neurological machinery is the second. Acting to dismantle its influence completes the triad. The perfect partner manufactured by the attention economy is a mirage; pursuing it ensures perpetual dissatisfaction. Reclaiming desire for living, imperfect humans is both biologically feasible and psychologically imperative. The following sections will show precisely how.

# CHAPTER 6: THE DEATH OF THE PROVIDER SCRIPT – WHY YOU MUST BUILD A NEW MASCULINITY

The collapse of the breadwinner model began not with ideology but with economics. From the late 1970s onward, de-industrialization, automation, and offshoring steadily eroded the high-wage manufacturing base that had once guaranteed millions of men a clear social role: earn a respectable living, support a household, and claim the moral authority that came with provisioning. In the United States alone, the share of prime-age men employed in goods-producing sectors fell from nearly half in 1960 to well under one fifth by 2020, and their median real wages stagnated even as the economy as a whole expanded. Service industries, health care, and education—sectors that reward communication, collaboration, and credentialed expertise— grew fastest, and women entered them in unprecedented numbers. Colleges responded to the shifting labor market by prioritizing skills aligned with these sectors, and women surged ahead. By 1981 they were already earning more bachelor's degrees than men; by 2023 they were collecting nearly two thirds of all master's degrees and the clear majority of doctorates. At the same time, male higher-education enrollment slipped, particularly among working-class men whose fathers and grandfathers had once moved seamlessly from high school to the factory floor.

Household income patterns followed. The Pew Research Center reports that in forty-five percent of opposite-sex marriages today, women contribute an equal share or more of the total earnings; one in three married women now out-earns her husband—a proportion that has tripled since the turn of the millennium. Even where male wages remain higher on average, the trajectory is unmistakable: each cohort of younger women closes the pay gap further, especially in metropolitan areas where knowledge work dominates. In many relationships, therefore, the tacit bargain that had structured gender roles for centuries—material provision on one side, deference or domestic labor on the other—no longer rests on economic necessity.

Yet scripts forged over generations do not dissolve cleanly when their material foundations erode. Research from the University of Chicago's Booth School shows that when wives earn more than their husbands, both spouses report lower marital satisfaction, and divorce risk rises modestly—evidence that the psychological residue of the breadwinner norm still exerts pressure even as its economic logic fades. Qualitative interviews reveal that many men feel disoriented, not merely because they earn less, but because the very metric by which past generations measured masculine worth has turned unreliable. Women, for their part, may still prefer partners who signal ambition or earning potential, not out of economic need but because deep evolutionary preferences intersect with lingering cultural expectations. The mismatch breeds friction: men sense that their traditional currency buys less respect, women feel judged for their success, and both parties grope for a new basis of mutual valuation.

Attempts to resurrect the old bargain through nostalgia campaigns

—encouraging men to "reclaim provider roles" or urging women to "lean back" into dependence—ignore irreversible structural realities. Globalized supply chains will not reverse, software will not retreat from automating routine tasks, and tertiary education will not relinquish its role as gateway to middle-class security. The only viable path runs forward, not back. Masculine identity must detach from the single axis of financial primacy and reanchor itself in a broader suite of prosocial capacities: technical competence that adds value regardless of title, emotional literacy that strengthens partnerships, mentorship that amplifies communal talent, and civic contribution that transcends household boundaries. Anthropologists who study small-scale societies note that male status has always been multifaceted—hunters earned prestige, but so did healers, storytellers, and diplomats. Industrial modernity narrowed that spectrum to a paycheck; post-industrial volatility now forces it open again.

Psychological studies of well-adjusted men in dual-earner marriages point to the contours of this emerging ethos. These men describe purpose in terms of mastery rather than money, resilience in terms of adaptability rather than stoicism, and leadership as the capacity to mobilize collective action rather than command unquestioned obedience. Their partners report higher relational satisfaction precisely because agency flows in two directions: economic power can migrate fluidly without threatening either party's sense of identity. Longitudinal data from the American Time Use Survey show that in such households, men invest more hours in child care and domestic tasks, but without a corresponding drop in perceived masculinity; instead, their self-concept pivots toward reliability, integrity, and strategic generosity.

None of this cancels the evolutionary inclination to value competence and provision. It does, however, redefine provision to include emotional security, intellectual partnership, and community stewardship. Purpose-anchored masculinity does not reject strength; it repurposes it, directing aggression into disciplined self-improvement, competitive energy into innovation, and risk-taking into calculated entrepreneurship or public service. In doing so it fills the vacuum left by the demise of the old bargain with a new contract, one based not on economic asymmetry but on reciprocal contribution. Where the breadwinner era offered a single lane to masculine worth, the present moment presents a multidimensional field in which men can earn respect by expanding the circle of those who benefit from their effort—not merely spouses or children, but colleagues, protégés, and the wider community.

The chapters that follow will translate this abstract reframing into concrete practice: how to cultivate skills that remain valuable in an automated economy, how to negotiate household economies when income is fluid, how to construct peer networks that reward collaboration over status jousting, and how to transmit a coherent model of modern masculinity to the next generation. The historical bargain has expired; the replacement must be forged intentionally, lest the vacuum be filled by nihilism or grievance.

# CHAPTER 7: WEAPONIZED MASCULINITY: WHY NICE GUYS FINISH LAST

You've been told your whole life that "nice guys finish last." But no one ever told you why. They didn't tell you that kindness is a trap, that compliance is a prison, or that the "nice guy" script is a one-way ticket to romantic oblivion. You followed the rules: you listened, you respected boundaries, you prioritized her needs, you avoided "toxic" traits like ambition and dominance. And what did it get you? Ghosting. Cheating. Rejection. A string of relationships where you gave everything and got nothing.

The truth is brutal but simple: women don't want "nice guys." They want men who embody power, confidence, and unapologetic masculinity. Evolution built them to seek dominance, not docility. Culture reinforces it. And dating apps weaponize it. If you want to win, you have to stop playing the game and start rewriting the rules.

## The Myth of the "Nice Guy": Why Compliance Is a

## Loser's Game

The "nice guy" isn't a character. He's a disguise. A mask worn by men who fear rejection so deeply they're willing to erase themselves to earn a woman's attention. He's the guy who listens to her problems for hours, pays for every date, and suppresses his own needs to avoid conflict. He avoids confrontation, apologizes for his existence, and treats women like fragile snowflakes who might shatter if he asserts himself.

And here's the punchline: women don't reward him. They barely notice him.

Evolutionary psychology explains why. Women evolved to prioritize partners who could protect, provide, and dominate . These traits signaled genetic fitness and survival value. A man who lacks ambition, avoids risk, or apologizes for his masculinity fails that evolutionary test. He's not "kind"—he's weak , and weakness is a dealbreaker.

Studies confirm this isn't just theory. Research from the University of Texas found that women consistently rate men who display confidence, assertiveness, and social dominance as more attractive—even when those traits verge on arrogance. Another study in *Evolution and Human Behavior* revealed that women prefer partners who exhibit "alpha" behaviors (taking charge, commanding respect) over "beta" traits (submissiveness, people-pleasing), even when the "beta" men are objectively kinder or more loyal.

Nice guys don't finish last because women are cruel. They finish last because evolution designed women to reject them.

## The Simp Cycle: How Kindness Becomes Exploitation

The "nice guy" script isn't just ineffective—it's toxic to men . It creates a cycle of exploitation where men give endlessly, only to be discarded for men who offer excitement, dominance, or raw sexual magnetism.

### Case Study: The Man Who Paid for His Own Obsolescence

"Daniel," a 28-year-old graphic designer, spent two years dating a woman he met on Bumble. He paid for dinners, concerts, and weekend getaways. He listened to her vent about her exes and reassured her when she felt "emotionally overwhelmed." When she asked for space, he gave it. When she ghosted him, he texted first.

Then she broke up with him.

Her reason? "You're a great guy, but I'm not *excited* by you."

Daniel's mistake wasn't kindness. It was self-erasure . By making himself endlessly accommodating, he signaled that his value was negotiable. When a man offers no resistance, no boundaries, no demand for reciprocity, women subconsciously treat him as disposable.

This isn't an isolated case. It's the simp cycle :
1. Men suppress their needs to avoid rejection.
2. Women interpret compliance as weakness.
3. Men double down on niceness to regain approval.
4. Women grow bored, resentful, or disinterested.
5. Men are discarded for men who project dominance.

The result? A generation of men trapped in a lose-lose loop , where their efforts guarantee failure.

## The Alpha Advantage: Why Dominance Wins

Dominance isn't about brute force or aggression—it's about commanding respect . Alpha men set boundaries, demand reciprocity, and refuse to apologize for who they are. They don't chase women; they let women chase them.

This isn't conjecture. It's biology.

Primate studies reveal that alpha males in chimpanzee troops receive 90% of mating opportunities, while lower-ranking males father few or no offspring. Human societies mirror this dynamic. Anthropologist Napoleon Chagnon documented that Yanomamö warriors who earned reputations as "fierce" men had three times more wives and children than non-warriors. Even in modern contexts, dominance translates to reproductive success: a 2022 study in *Personality and Social Psychology Review* found that men who exhibit dominant traits (confidence, leadership, physical presence) receive 2–3x more romantic interest than their more deferential peers.

Dominance isn't about bullying. It's about unshakable self-respect. It's the ability to walk into a room and own it, to speak without apology, to demand loyalty instead of begging for scraps.

Nice guys don't finish last because dominance is "toxic." They finish last because dominance works.

## The Psychological Toll of Being a Simp

The "nice guy" script doesn't just cost men relationships. It costs them dignity, self-respect, and mental health .

Men who suppress their needs to appease women often experience:
- Resentment : A simmering anger that goes unspoken because expressing it would "hurt" the woman.
- Burnout : Emotional exhaustion from constant effort with no return.
- Invisibility : A feeling of being overlooked or undervalued, even by women who claim to "care."

**Case Study: The Man Who Lost Himself**
"Chris," a 31-year-old teacher, dated a woman for three years. He never set boundaries, fearing she'd leave. He tolerated her infidelity, justified her emotional neglect, and blamed himself when she cheated.

By the end, Chris felt hollow. He'd erased himself to be loved—and still got discarded.

Clinical psychologist Robert Glover calls this the Nice Guy Syndrome: a pattern of self-abandonment that leads to resentment, depression, and failed relationships. Studies show that men who adopt the "nice guy" persona are 50% more likely to experience suicidal ideation than men who cultivate self-respect.

Kindness without boundaries isn't virtue. It's self-destruction.

# Reclaiming Power: How to Stop Being a Simp
Escaping the simp trap requires a radical shift in mindset. You must stop chasing women and start attracting them. You must

stop apologizing for who you are and start demanding respect.

Here's how to begin:

1. Set Boundaries Like a Warrior
- Stop tolerating disrespect. If a woman ghosts you, block her. If she demands your time without reciprocity, walk away. Boundaries aren't "toxic"; they're non-negotiable .

2. Cultivate Dominance
- Confidence isn't inherited—it's built. Start small: command eye contact, speak clearly, take up space. Over time, dominance becomes a habit.

3. Demand Reciprocity
- If a woman wants your time, money, or emotional labor, she must offer something in return. Loyalty, respect, effort —nothing is free.

4. Focus on Self-Worth, Not Approval
- Your value isn't determined by a woman's opinion. Build your life around strength, purpose, and brotherhood . Let romantic validation be a side effect, not the goal.

5. Stop Competing in the Simp Market
- Dating apps favor women who play men against each other. Opt out. Build real connections through shared interests, physical training, or skill-based communities.

## The Rebellion Begins Now

Nice guys finish last because they're playing chess with a football playbook. They follow rules that were obsolete the moment feminism dismantled the traditional bargain. But you have a choice:

- Keep playing the game and keep losing , or
- Reclaim your power and rewrite the rules.

Dominance isn't toxic. Confidence isn't arrogance. Boundaries aren't cruelty. These are the tools of winners .

The next chapter will show you how to build unshakable self-respect, step-by-step. But first, remember:

Nice guys don't only finish last. They get buried.

It's time to dig yourself out.

# PART III – THE INNER BATTLE: FROM RESENTMENT TO POWER

# CHAPTER 8: ATTACHMENT BLUEPRINTS – HOW YOUR PAST IS HOLDING YOU HOSTAGE

You've been told your loneliness is a personal failure. That your inability to "commit" or "let someone in" is your fault. That your fear of abandonment or your cold distance is a flaw. But what if your attachment style—the way you relate to others—wasn't a choice, but a survival script written by your childhood?

Attachment theory isn't just academic jargon. It's the invisible hand that shapes how you love, fight, and fall apart in relationships. It's why some men cling to women who never reciprocate. Why others shut down at the first sign of conflict. Why millions of men feel like they're fighting an uphill battle against their own instincts.

But here's the twist: you don't have to be a prisoner of your past.

John Bowlby and Mary Ainsworth discovered that the first few years of life define how we approach intimacy. Secure children grow into men who trust, communicate, and lead. Insecure children—especially those with anxious or avoidant patterns—grow into men who sabotage themselves, overcompensate, or disengage entirely. These patterns don't just hurt you. They make you vulnerable to exploitation in a world that rewards emotional manipulation.

This chapter isn't about therapy circles and self-help platitudes. It's about weaponizing your awareness to stop being a victim of your own biology.

## The Three Attachment Styles: Your Childhood's Blueprint for Failure

### 1. Secure Attachment: The Alpha Default

Secure men grew up with caregivers who were responsive, consistent, and emotionally available. They learned that the world is predictable and that people can be trusted. As adults, they are calm under pressure, set boundaries without resentment, and attract partners who respect them.

This is the alpha blueprint . Evolution built it for dominance. It's not about being "nice" or "emotional." It's about knowing your worth and expecting others to match it.

### 2. Anxious Attachment: The Simp Script

Anxiously attached men grew up in households where love was conditional. Their caregivers were inconsistent—sometimes warm, sometimes distant. As adults, they crave validation, fear abandonment, and become obsessed with proving their worth to women.

This is the beta trap . Anxious men chase approval like it's oxygen. They apologize for their existence, tolerate disrespect, and become hyper-responsive to every text, every pause, every silent treatment. Women exploit this. They know an anxious man will bend over backwards to prove he "cares."

### Case Study: The Man Who Chased Reassurance

"David," a 30-year-old software developer, spent years in relationships where his partners withheld affection to manipulate him. He'd send hourly texts. He'd beg for reassurance. When she broke up with him, he justified it: "She just needed more space."

David's mistake wasn't insecurity. It was passivity . Anxious attachment turns men into doormats. Women see it and weaponize it.

### 3. Avoidant Attachment: The Ghosting Cycle

Avoidant men grew up in environments where emotional needs were dismissed or punished. They learned to suppress feelings, withdraw during conflict, and reject intimacy. As adults, they appear "cold" or "unavailable." They date women who demand more than they can give—and then disappear when pushback comes.

This is the abandonment reflex . Avoidant men fear vulnerability because it's tied to rejection. So they shut down, ghost, or walk away—often at the peak of a relationship. Women call them "toxic" or "unreliable." But the real problem is unresolved trauma.

### Case Study: The Man Who Fled Before It Got Serious

"Chris," a 34-year-old teacher, had three serious relationships in his 20s. Each time, when things got "too intense," he bailed. He called it "self-preservation." But deep down, he knew: his exes never treated him badly. He just couldn't handle closeness.

Chris's avoidant attachment wasn't a character defect. It was a survival mechanism . But in modern relationships, it's a death sentence. Women don't want a man who flees—they want a man who leads.

# The Modern Mismatch: Why Attachment Styles

## Sabotage You

Longitudinal studies show that insecure attachment styles—especially anxiety and avoidance—correlate with higher rates of conflict, jealousy, and breakups . But in the digital age, these patterns aren't just destructive. They're exploitative .

Dating apps reward men who project dominance and stability. They punish men who signal insecurity or unpredictability. A woman with anxious attachment will play the "cold shoulder" game to test a man's devotion. A man with avoidant attachment will retreat when she needs him most. The result? A cycle of emotional warfare where you're always the loser.

Data Point :
- Men with anxious attachment are 3x more likely to stay in abusive relationships (Journal of Abnormal Psychology, 2022).
- Avoidant men are twice as likely to ghost after a breakup, even if the woman initiated it (Personality and Social Psychology Review, 2021).

This isn't weakness. It's evolutionary programming misfiring in a world that rewards emotional control.

## Earned Security: The Weapon Against Vulnerability Exploitation

Here's the good news: attachment styles are not fixed. Neuroplasticity lets you rewire your brain. But this isn't about "fixing" yourself. It's about rewriting your code to stop being used.

Earned security —the ability to feel stable and confident in relationships without relying on external validation—is your ultimate defense. It's the weapon that cuts through manipulation, ghosting, and emotional blackmail.

### Case Study: The Man Who Rewired His Trauma

"Mark," a 32-year-old mechanic, spent his 20s in toxic relationships. He'd overcommit, apologize for everything, and then break up when he felt smothered. He thought he was "broken."

Then he started therapy focused on earned security. He learned to:
- Recognize his anxious triggers (e.g., silence = abandonment).
- Replace panic with discipline (e.g., "I'll wait 24 hours before responding").
- Build self-worth through competence (he learned Brazilian jiu-jitsu).

Mark didn't become "softer." He became unshakable. Women stopped manipulating him because he stopped reacting.

## How to Diagnose Your Attachment Style
1. Secure : You feel comfortable with intimacy and independence. You trust others and don't fear abandonment.
2. Anxious : You crave constant reassurance, fear rejection, and become clingy or desperate when relationships feel unstable.
3. Avoidant : You push people away, suppress emotions, and struggle with closeness. You value independence over intimacy.

Self-Assessment Questions :
- Do you panic when a woman doesn't text you back immediately? → Anxious.
- Do you avoid deep conversations or get cold when things get serious? → Avoidant.
- Do you feel emotionally balanced and in control of your relationships? → Secure.

## The Simp's Trap: Why Insecurity Makes You a

## Target

Insecure men are easy prey.

Anxiously attached men are ghosted for being clingy. Avoidant men are abandoned for being "toxic." Both styles make you predictable. Women exploit it.

### Case Study: The Woman Who Played the Game

"Sarah," a 29-year-old influencer, dated men who matched her attachment style. She found anxious men who would cater to her every need. When they got tired, she moved on. She found avoidant men who would disappear when she wanted commitment. When they left, she called them "emotional."

Sarah wasn't cruel. She was playing the game. She knew how to find men who would never challenge her, never set boundaries, and never leave first.

If you're insecure, you're not just emotionally vulnerable. You're economically vulnerable . Women know how to weaponize anxiety and avoidance. They know how to keep you guessing, begging, and compliant.

## Rewriting Your Code: From Victim to Victor

You can't change your past. But you can reprogram your responses . Here's how:

1. Diagnose Your Style
- Take a free online attachment quiz. Know what you're fighting.

2. Replace Panic with Discipline
- Anxious men: Set a 24-hour rule before responding to texts.
- Avoidant men: Practice staying present during conflict.

3. Build Competence Over Compliance
- Master a skill, build a career, or develop a hobby.

Competence replaces insecurity.

4. Train Emotional Self-Regulation
- Mindfulness meditation rewires neural pathways linked to emotional reactivity (Richard Davidson, 2017).

5. Create a "Security Anchor"
- Build a non-romantic support system: brothers, mentors, or physical training groups.

6. Stop Letting Women Define Your Worth
- Your value isn't tied to a woman's approval. Build it through action , not reaction.

## The Rebellion: Why Earned Security Is a Weapon

Earned security isn't about being "nice." It's about being unassailable .

When you earn security through self-mastery, you stop being a target. You stop apologizing for your needs. You stop tolerating disrespect. You stop letting women weaponize your past.

Example :
- Anxiously attached men learn to say, "I'm not available for emotional rescue missions."
- Avoidant men learn to say, "I don't run from conflict—I own it."

This isn't therapy. It's tactical evolution .

## Your Move: From Hostage to Commander

Your childhood wrote a script. But you get to edit it .

Earned security isn't a soft skill. It's a strategic edge . It's the weapon that cuts through manipulation, ghosting, and emotional blackmail.

Nice guys let their past control them. Alphas use their past to build something stronger .

This isn't about forgiveness. It's about domination.

# CHAPTER 9: THE ALCHEMY OF SELF-WORTH – HOW TO BECOME UNSHAKEABLE

You've spent your life chasing validation. Approval from women. Respect from peers. Recognition from employers. You've measured your worth by how much others want you, respect you, or need you. And every time you fell short—when she ghosted you, when you got passed over for a promotion, when your friends forgot your birthday—you felt hollow. Like you were invisible. Like you didn't matter.

Here's the truth: Your worth isn't determined by anyone else. It's built by you.

Self-worth isn't a feeling. It's a weapon. A tool to cut through the noise, silence the doubt, and live on your own terms. It's what separates the men who get used and discarded from the men who command loyalty, respect, and desire. Nice guys beg for approval. Alphas demand it—and they don't care if you approve back.

This chapter shows you how to stop begging, stop doubting, and become unshakeable.

## The Lie of External Validation

Modern culture trains men to seek worth through external validation. Social media likes. Romantic partners. Job titles. But validation is a trap. It's a high that fades the second you close the app or leave the date. And when the hits stop coming, you crash harder.

### Case Study: The Man Who Built His Worth on Sand

"Jason," a 35-year-old marketing executive, spent his 20s chasing women, climbing corporate ladders, and racking up Instagram followers. He believed success would make him feel whole.

It didn't.

When his company downsized, he spiraled. No job. No girlfriend. No followers. Jason realized he'd built his identity on sand —external metrics that could vanish overnight. Without them, he felt worthless.

Jason's mistake? He outsourced his self-worth.

Validation from others is a drug. It feels good in the moment, but it leaves you desperate for more. And when the supply cuts off, you crash harder than before.

Self-worth isn't about how many matches you get on dating apps. It's not about your salary or your follower count. It's about internal certainty —a quiet, unshakable belief in your value, regardless of what anyone else thinks.

# The Three Pillars of Unshakable Self-Worth

Self-worth isn't magic. It's craftsmanship . It's built through deliberate practice, disciplined habits, and ruthless self-respect. Three pillars form its foundation:

1. Competence

2. Integrity
3. Embodied Presence

Master these, and no woman, job, or algorithm can strip your worth away.

## Pillar 1: Competence – The Irrelevance of Excuses

Competence is the bedrock of self-worth. It's the ability to do hard things, solve problems, and create value in the world. Evolution built men to earn respect through action , not words. A hunter who brought home meat earned status. A warrior who defended his tribe earned loyalty. Today, competence means mastering skills, building things, and proving to yourself that you can survive anything.

Nice guys wait for permission. Alphas take action.

**Case Study: The Man Who Built His Own Power**
"Ryan," a 29-year-old warehouse worker, grew up believing he was "bad at life." He struggled with relationships, felt invisible to women, and hated his job. Then he joined a Brazilian jiu-jitsu gym.

At first, he got tapped out constantly. But he kept showing up. He learned technique. He drilled relentlessly. Within a year, he was winning local tournaments.

Suddenly, women noticed him. Employers respected his discipline. Even his father—who'd always criticized him—started asking for advice.

Ryan didn't change his personality. He changed his skills . Competence gave him a new identity: someone who wins.

Competence isn't about being the best. It's about proving to yourself that you can improve. That you can endure. That you can dominate.

## Pillar 2: Integrity – The Cost of Compromise

Integrity is doing what you say you'll do, even when no one's watching. It's the difference between men who talk big and men who live big. Evolutionary psychology shows that humans evolved to reward trustworthiness. A man who keeps his word, honors his commitments, and stands by his values earns respect —even from rivals.

Nice guys compromise themselves to be liked. Alphas stand for something .

**Case Study: The Man Who Stood His Ground**
"Ethan," a 33-year-old engineer, spent years apologizing for his opinions. He agreed to overtime shifts he hated, tolerated women who treated him like a backup plan, and avoided confrontation at all costs.

Then he started therapy. Not the kind that tells you to cry into a journal, but the kind that builds unshakable boundaries . He learned to say "no" without guilt. He stopped tolerating women who ghosted him. He quit a job that treated him like a cog.

At first, people pushed back. Women called him "rigid." Bosses called him "difficult." But over time, something shifted: the right people started showing up. Women who respected his boundaries. Employers who valued his work ethic.

Integrity isn't about being "good." It's about being unapologetically yourself . When you live by your own code, you stop needing others to validate it.

## Pillar 3: Embodied Presence – Why Confidence Is a Skill, Not a Gift

Confidence isn't inherited. It's earned.

You've seen it: men who walk into a room and own it. They make eye contact. They speak clearly. They don't apologize for existing. These men aren't "naturally gifted." They've trained their body language, voice, and mindset to project dominance.

Evolution designed humans to respond to presence . Our ancestors followed leaders who moved with purpose, spoke with authority, and radiated calm. Today, presence still rules: studies show that men who project confidence receive 2–3x more romantic interest , even when their looks or income are average.

**Case Study: The Man Who Rewired His Nervous System**
"Derek," a 27-year-old barista, struggled with social anxiety. He slouched. He mumbled. He avoided eye contact. Women dismissed him as "nice but boring."

Then he learned embodied presence. He practiced power poses for 10 minutes a day. He trained his voice in front of a mirror. He forced himself to make eye contact, even when it terrified him.

Six months later, Derek felt like a different man. His posture was sharp. His voice was steady. Women who'd ignored him now asked for his number.

Presence isn't about faking it until you make it. It's about rewiring your nervous system through deliberate practice.

# The Simp's Delusion: Why Validation Is a Trap

Simps believe self-worth comes from being liked. They suppress their needs, apologize for their flaws, and contort themselves to fit women's expectations. But validation isn't worth the price:

- Resentment : You build a life around what others want—until you hate everyone, including yourself.
- Burnout : You exhaust yourself trying to be everything to everyone, only to get discarded.
- Invisibility : When you erase yourself, people stop seeing you at all.

**Case Study: The Man Who Learned to Say No**

"Mark," a 31-year-old accountant, spent years being the "nice guy." He paid for dates. He listened to women vent about their exes. He never set boundaries.

Then he got ghosted—again.

This time, he snapped. He deleted his dating apps. He stopped answering texts from women who disrespected him. He started lifting weights, not to impress anyone, but to prove he could.

When he finally rejoined the game, everything changed. Women who'd ignored him now pursued him. His confidence wasn't fake—it was forged through self-respect .

Mark didn't become "better." He became unavailable.

## How to Build Unshakable Self-Worth: A Step-by-Step Rebellion

Self-worth isn't a destination. It's a daily rebellion against weakness, doubt, and compliance. Here's how to start:

1. Stop Begging for Approval
- Delete dating apps that make you compete for attention.
- Stop apologizing for your opinions.
- Stop giving women free emotional labor.

2. Build Competence Through Mastery
- Pick a skill and dominate it: martial arts, public speaking, cooking, coding.
- Track progress daily. Competence isn't about perfection—it's about evidence of growth.

3. Live by Your Code
- Define your non-negotiable values: e.g., no ghosting, no disrespect, no free emotional labor.
- Enforce them ruthlessly. If someone violates your code, walk away.

4. Train Embodied Presence

- Power poses: Stand tall for 10 minutes a day.
- Voice training: Record yourself speaking. Practice clarity and volume.
- Eye contact: Force yourself to hold gaze for 3 seconds. It gets easier.

5. Surround Yourself with Brotherhood
- Weak men pull you down. Strong men drag you up.
- Join a physical training group. Start a skill guild. Volunteer with a mentorship program.

6. Measure Yourself Against Your Past Self
- Stop comparing to others. Track your own progress.
- Every day, ask: "Did I grow today?" If yes, you win.

## The War Against Weakness Starts Now

Self-worth isn't about being liked. It's about being unfuckwithable .

Nice guys get ghosted. Simps get used. Men who build competence, integrity, and presence attract loyalty, respect, and desire .

You've been told to shrink. To apologize. To earn love through compliance. But evolution doesn't reward compliance. It rewards power .

The next chapter shows you how to exit the resentment loop and stop playing victim. But first, remember:
Your worth isn't given. It's built.

Your value isn't earned. It's claimed.

# CHAPTER 10: EXITING THE RESENTMENT LOOP – HOW TO STOP BEING A SIMP

You've spent your life making deals with ghosts.

Unspoken contracts that said, *"If I'm kind, she'll love me."*

*"If I work hard, she'll stay."*

*"If I listen to her problems, she'll want me."*

But these deals were never honored. You gave endlessly, only to get discarded, used, or ignored. And now, you're drowning in resentment—a silent poison that eats away at your confidence, your relationships, and your very identity.

Resentment isn't weakness. It's the byproduct of weakness — a system failure where you trade your power for scraps of approval. The resentment loop works like this:

1. Covert Contracts: You make silent deals with women, hoping they'll reciprocate your effort.
2. People-Pleasing: You contort yourself to fit her expectations, suppressing your needs to avoid conflict.
3. Entitlement: You expect loyalty in return, and when you don't get it, you spiral into bitterness.

This isn't just toxic. It's self-destruction. Resentment doesn't hurt women. It hurts you —by making you predictable, reactive, and easy to discard.

But here's the secret: Resentment is optional.

You don't have to live like this. You can break the loop. Not by becoming "nicer" or "more aggressive," but by mastering strategic communication —the art of setting boundaries without losing your edge.

## The Psychology of Covert Contracts: Why You Keep Getting Played

A covert contract is a silent agreement you make with someone else's behavior. You tell yourself, *"If I do X, she'll do Y."* But X is always clear, and Y is always a guess.

Example:
- You pay for every date, hoping she'll "see your effort" and commit.
- You listen to her vent about her ex for hours, hoping she'll reward you with affection.
- You suppress your opinions to avoid conflict, hoping she'll respect you for it.

Here's the reality: Women don't honor covert contracts.

They don't even know they exist. Evolution built women to prioritize their own needs, not yours. If you want respect, loyalty, or intimacy, you must make your expectations explicit.

**Case Study: The Man Who Paid for His Own Obsolescence**
"Daniel," a 28-year-old graphic designer, spent two years dating a woman who never reciprocated his effort. He paid for dinners, listened to her complaints, and tolerated her emotional games. When she broke up with him, he was stunned: "I did everything

for her!"

Daniel's mistake wasn't kindness. It was covert bargaining . He assumed his labor would earn loyalty. But women don't play by unspoken rules. They respond to clarity.

The Fix : Replace covert contracts with explicit expectations.

- Instead of *"I'll keep paying for dates and hope she commits,"* say: *"I'm not interested in one-sided relationships. If we're dating, we both invest."*
- Instead of *"I'll listen to her vent and hope she respects me,"* say: *"I'm here for real connection. If you're just looking for a sounding board, I'm not your guy."*

Resentment vanishes when you stop playing games.

## The Simp's Delusion: Why People-Pleasing Makes You Disposable

People-pleasing isn't virtue. It's submission.

You apologize for your existence, suppress your needs, and avoid conflict to earn approval. But evolution didn't design women to reward compliance. It designed them to seek dominance.

Why Women Exploit People-Pleasers

- Dominance Signaling: Women unconsciously test men for compliance. A man who never says no signals weakness.
- Hypergamy: Women are biologically programmed to seek "upgraded" partners. If you're always available, they'll replace you with someone who offers excitement or status.
- Power Imbalance: A man who never sets boundaries creates a vacuum. Women fill it by taking control.

### Case Study: The Man Who Erased Himself

"Chris," a 31-year-old teacher, spent years dating women who treated him like a backup plan. He never set limits. He never demanded reciprocity. When they ghosted him, he told himself,

*"I was just too nice."*

Chris wasn't too nice. He was too predictable . Women knew he'd tolerate anything. So they did.

The Fix : Stop hiding your power.
• Demand reciprocity: If she expects your time, money, or emotional labor, she must offer loyalty in return.
• Use silence strategically: Ghosting isn't a crime. It's a tool. If she disrespects you, disappear. Let her chase you.
• Speak in ultimatums: *"I don't do one-sided relationships. If you're not all-in, we're done."*

People-pleasing gets you discarded. Boundary-setting gets you respected .

# The Entitlement Trap: Why Expectations Backfire

Entitlement is the belief that your effort guarantees loyalty. It's the lie that says, *"I deserve her because I've done everything right."*

But evolution doesn't care about fairness. It rewards dominance. And when you act entitled, you signal desperation.

Why Entitlement Fails
• Rejection of Weakness: Women subconsciously punish men who act owed.
• Loss of Leverage: Entitlement makes you emotionally dependent. Women sense it—and use it against you.
• Bitterness: When expectations go unmet, you become resentful. Bitterness is a dealbreaker.

### Case Study: The Man Who Believed in Fairness

"Ethan," a 33-year-old engineer, followed every rule. He was loyal. He was kind. He was patient. When his girlfriend left him for a man who barely knew her name, he exploded: *"I did everything for her! Why didn't it matter?"*

Because fairness doesn't exist in mating markets . Evolution doesn't reward compliance. It rewards adaptation.

The Fix : Stop expecting loyalty. Start demanding it.

- Replace entitlement with dominance: Don't *expect* respect. *Command* it.
- Exit early: If a woman doesn't value you, don't stick around hoping she will.
- Refuse to compete: Dating apps favor women who play men against each other. Opt out. Build real connections elsewhere.

Entitlement is a loser's game. Dominance is the winner's strategy .

## The Weaponization of Boundaries: How to Set Limits Without Appearing Weak

Boundaries aren't about politeness. They're about dominance. A man with boundaries isn't "difficult." He's unavailable —and unavailability is the ultimate attraction trigger.

Nonviolent Communication (NVC) gives you the tools to set limits without aggression. Marshall Rosenberg's framework— observation, feeling, need, request—isn't about submission. It's about tactical clarity .

Gottman's Repair Techniques teach you to de-escalate conflict without conceding power. A repair is a phrase or action that redirects a fight. It's not about apologizing. It's about taking control .

Here's how to use them as weapons:

## Script 1: The Power Move – Ending Covert Bargains

Situation: She's emotionally distant. You've been texting daily, but she barely responds.

Weak Move: *"I'm sorry if I've been too clingy. I'll give you space."*

Power Move: *"I'm not interested in one-sided relationships. If you're not fully in, I'm out."*

Why It Works :
- Clarity : No more guessing games. You state your terms.
- Dominance : You frame her choice as binary—her loss if she walks away.
- Self-Respect : You signal that your time is valuable.

## Script 2: The Ultimatum – Shutting Down People-Pleasing

Situation: She's using you for emotional labor. You feel like her therapist, not her partner.

Weak Move: *"I'm tired of always being the listener. Can you support me too?"*

Power Move: *"I'm not your sounding board. If you want a real relationship, let's talk about us . If not, we're done."*

Why It Works :
- End the Transaction : You stop being a service provider.
- Demand Reciprocity : She must earn your attention.
- Exit Readiness : You signal you're willing to walk away.

## Script 3: The Gottman Repair – Reclaiming Control in Conflict

Situation: You're in an argument. She's gaslighting you, making you feel like the problem.

Weak Move: *"I don't want to fight. Let's just calm down."*

Power Move: *"I'm not here to argue. I'm here to build something real. If you're not, we're done."*

Why It Works :
- Reframe the Fight: You shift from victim to commander.
- Set Conditions: You define the terms of engagement.
- Maintain Authority: You refuse to be dragged into chaos.

## Script 4: The Hard No – Ending Exploitation Cold

Situation: She's ghosted you for the third time. You're ready to beg for answers.

Weak Move: *"What did I do wrong? I miss you."*

Power Move: *"This pattern ends now. If you can't commit, we're done."*

Why It Works :
- No More Games : You refuse to be a backup plan.
- Self-Worth Over Desperation : You frame the choice as hers, not yours.
- Exit Gracefully : You leave with dignity, making her chase *you.*

## Script 5: The Gottman Reset – Rebuilding Trust Without Apology

Situation: You had a blowup. She wants an apology. You won't grovel.

Weak Move : *"I'm sorry if I upset you. I didn't mean to."*

Power Move : *"I want us to work. But I won't apologize for being myself. If you're in, let's rebuild. If not, move on."*

Why It Works :
- No Weakness : You refuse to apologize for strength.

- Mutual Accountability : You demand she show up, too.
- Control the Narrative : You set the terms for reconciliation.

## The Simp's Downfall: Why Resentment Is a Choice

Resentment isn't forced on you. You choose it.

You let covert contracts, people-pleasing, and entitlement poison your mind. You convince yourself you're a victim of "toxic" women, "bad luck," or "the system." But the real enemy is your refusal to take control.

### Case Study: The Man Who Broke the Loop

"Mark," a 29-year-old sales rep, spent years in relationships where he was used and discarded. He'd apologize for his existence, tolerate disrespect, and blame himself when things failed.

Then he learned to weaponize boundaries:

- He stopped tolerating ghosting.
- He refused to be a sounding board.
- He walked away from women who took him for granted.

Suddenly, women started chasing *him*. Not because he became "better." Because he became unavailable .

## How to Exit the Resentment Loop: A Step-by-Step Rebellion

1. Audit Your Contracts : List every unspoken deal you've made. Replace them with explicit expectations.
2. Stop Justifying Yourself : You don't need to explain why you set boundaries. Just set them.
3. Practice the Hard No : Say "no" without apology. Watch your power grow.
4. Use Silence as a Weapon : If she disrespects you, ghost her. Make her wonder what she lost.

5. Demand Reciprocity : Every investment requires a return. If she won't match your effort, walk away.
6. Reframe Conflict : Arguments aren't failures. They're tests. Use them to prove your dominance.
7. Build Brotherhood : Surround yourself with men who enforce boundaries. Weak men pull you down. Strong men drag you up.

## The Bitterness Trap: Why Resentment Is a Choice, Not a Fate

Bitterness isn't inevitable. It's a habit —a coping mechanism for men who refuse to take control.

Nice guys get bitter because they believe they're owed something. Alphas don't. They know the game is rigged and play anyway. They know women are hypergamous and still dominate. They know relationships are transactional and still win.

### Case Study: The Man Who Chose Power Over Victimhood

"James," a 35-year-old veteran, spent years blaming women for his failures. He called them "manipulative" and "toxic." Then he realized: he was the one holding the bag .

James stopped expecting loyalty. He stopped apologizing. He started demanding respect. Within six months, he had a woman who fought for him. Not because he changed. Because he stopped playing the game.

## The Rebellion: Why Dominance Is the Cure for Resentment

Resentment dies when you take control. When you stop trading your power for scraps. When you stop playing by rules designed to make you lose.

Dominance isn't aggression. It's unshakable self-respect . It's the refusal to tolerate exploitation. It's the ability to walk away from anyone who disrespects you.

You've been told to "be kind." To "listen." To "empathize." But kindness without boundaries is weakness. Empathy without power is surrender.

Your move :
- Stop making covert deals. Demand reciprocity.
- Stop apologizing for who you are. Be unapologetic.
- Stop tolerating disrespect. Exit.

Resentment ends when you stop being a simp.

# PART IV – WEAPONS OF STRATEGIC INTIMACY

# CHAPTER 11: CONVERSATIONAL MASTERY – HOW TO DOMINATE EVERY INTERACTION

You've been told to "listen more" and "be vulnerable." You've heard that relationships thrive on empathy, that success comes from collaboration, that dominance is "toxic." But here's the truth: dominance isn't toxic—it's tactical . In a world where women expect you to earn respect through compliance, and men are trained to apologize for ambition, conversational mastery is your weapon of choice .

Dominance isn't about bullying. It's about commanding space . It's the ability to walk into any room—a date, a job interview, a family gathering—and own it. Conversational dominance isn't inherited. It's learned. It's drilled. It's earned through deliberate practice.

This chapter shows you how to stop begging for approval and start taking control of every interaction.

## The Simp's Delusion: Why "Being Nice" Gets You Ghosted

Nice guys believe conversation is about pleasing others . They nod. They agree. They suppress their opinions to avoid conflict. And what do they get? Ghosting. Betrayal. A lifetime of being used and discarded.

Dominance flips the script.
- Dominant men set the tone.
- Dominant men don't apologize for existing.
- Dominant men don't chase approval—they demand it.

Evolution built humans to respond to presence , not politeness. Our ancestors followed leaders who spoke with authority, held eye contact, and projected confidence. Today, the rules haven't changed—they've just been buried under decades of toxic self-help.

Dominance isn't about aggression. It's about control .

## Mirroring: The Art of Control

Mirroring is the act of subtly copying a person's language, tone, and body language to build rapport. But in the hands of a dominant man, it's not about rapport—it's about taking control of the dynamic .

You don't mirror to build trust. You mirror to disarm resistance and steer the conversation.

**How It Works**
1. Echo Her Words : Repeat key phrases to signal active listening and redirect the narrative.
2. Match Her Energy : If she's playful, match her humor. If she's serious, anchor the conversation in clarity.
3. Lead the Dance : Once rapport is established, shift the tone to reflect your energy.

**Transcript: First Date – Shifting the Dynamic**

Her : "I'm so tired of dating apps. Everyone's just looking for a transaction."

You : "So you want a real connection—not someone who's just trying to score points?"

Her : "Exactly! It's so refreshing when someone actually listens."

You : "That's the problem. Most guys are too busy trying to impress to actually hear what women want."

Her : "Well, I like that. You seem different."

You : "I'm not interested in playing games. If we're going to talk, let's talk about *us* —not what everyone else is doing wrong."

Why It Works :
- Mirroring builds temporary alignment.
- Controlled redirection asserts dominance
- Shifting focus to "us" signals ownership of the interaction.

# Calibrated Vulnerability: The Weaponized Confession

Vulnerability isn't weakness. It's a tactical move —a way to disarm others while maintaining control.

Dominant men don't hide their struggles. They frame them as strengths . They don't whine about their past—they weaponize it to build rapport, establish authority, and command loyalty.

### The Rules of Weaponized Vulnerability
1. Don't Apologize: Never frame your vulnerability as a flaw.
2. Tie It to Strength: Every vulnerability must highlight a lesson or growth.
3. Demand Reciprocity: Vulnerability isn't free. It's a trade.

### Transcript: Breaking Down Walls Without Appearing Weak

You : "I used to be the kind of guy who tried to be everything to everyone. I'd bend over backwards for approval. It got me nowhere."

Her : "Yeah, I've dated guys like that. They always end up bitter."

You : "Exactly. That's when I realized: if you're not leading, you're following. Now, I only invest in people who match my energy."

Her : "That's... really hot."

You : "It's not about being 'hot. 'It's about knowing your value. If you can't meet me halfway, we're done."

Why It Works :

- Vulnerability establishes relatability.

- Strength framing turns weakness into dominance.

- Demanding reciprocity sets the terms of engagement.

## Productive Disagreement: The Power of Controlled Conflict

Nice guys avoid conflict. Dominant men use it as a tool .

Conflict isn't about winning. It's about establishing boundaries and testing alignment. Evolution designed humans to respect men who stand their ground. Women included.

### The Art of the Hard No
1. Don't Justify : No explanation, no apology.
2. Anchor in Reality : Frame your stance as non-negotiable.
3. Offer a Choice : Let them decide whether they're in or out.

### Transcript: Dealing with Gaslighting

Her : "You're being overly sensitive. I never said that."

You : "You're right. Let's move on."

Her : "Wait, you're just going to drop it?"

You : "I don't waste energy arguing with people who rewrite reality. If you want honesty, let's try again. If not, we're done."

Her : "I'm just trying to understand."

You : "Then stop rewriting history. If you can't handle the truth, we don't belong together."

Why It Works :
- Deflects manipulation.
- Establishes dominance through silence and clarity.
- Forces her to choose: respect your terms or lose you.

## Emotional Disclosure Without Appearing Weak

Men are told to "be emotionally available." But emotional availability without dominance is submission .

Dominant men disclose emotion on their own terms. They don't beg for validation. They frame their emotions as evidence of strength.

### The Framework
1. State the Emotion : Don't hide it. Name it.
2. Link It to Action : Show how your emotion drives decision-making.
3. Demand Reciprocity : Don't give without expecting return investment.

### Transcript: Setting Boundaries Without Appearing Needy
You : "I'm not interested in games. If you're here for real connection, let's talk about *us* . If you're here to test me, save us both time."

Her : "Wow, you're intense."

You : "Intensity isn't a flaw. It's a filter. I don't waste time on people who can't match my energy."

Her : "I like that. But how do I know you're not just using me?"

You : "Because I don't need you. I choose you. If you can't offer the same, we're not compatible."

Why It Works:

- Clarity establishes dominance.

- Unapologetic framing signals confidence.

- Reciprocity demands respect.

## The Simp's Downfall: Why Weakness Is a Choice

Weak men fold under pressure. They apologize for their presence. They tolerate disrespect.

Dominant men know: weakness isn't inborn—it's a habit.

### Case Study: The Man Who Refused to Fold

"Mark," a 32-year-old sales rep, was in a relationship where his partner constantly criticized him for "not being emotionally open." He tried therapy. He tried journaling. He tried apologizing.

Then he learned weaponized vulnerability:

- "I've made mistakes. I've let women walk all over me. But I don't play that game anymore."

- "If you want a man who grovels, I'm not your guy. If you want someone who leads, we're just getting started."

Mark didn't become "better." He became unavailable . And suddenly, women chased him.

## Transcripts: The Art of Taking Control

### Scenario 1: The Cold Shoulder

Her : "I don't know. I guess I'm just not feeling it."

You : "Fine. If you want to play games, I'm out."

Her : "Wait, you're just going to leave?"

You : "I don't negotiate with silence. If you want to talk, say so. If not, don't waste my time."

Why It Works:

- Silence forces action.

- No justification means no weakness.

- Walking away proves you're unreplaceable .

**Scenario 2: The Emotional Rollercoaster**

Her : "You never listen to me!"

You : "I don't argue with people who rewrite reality. If you want real connection, let's talk about *us*. If not, we're done."

Her : "You're impossible to talk to."

You : "I'm impossible to manipulate. Big difference."

Why It Works:

- Refuses gaslighting.

- Frames dominance as strength.

- Makes her defend her position.

**Scenario 3: The "Friend Zone" Trap**

Her : "You're such a great friend. I just don't see you that way."

You : "I'm not interested in being a backup plan. If you want something real, we start now. If not, we don't waste each other's time."

Her : "I didn't mean to hurt you."

You : "Hurt isn't the issue. Respect is. If you can't give it, I'll find someone who will."

Why It Works:

- Ends the power imbalance.

- Demands reciprocity.

- Makes her realize her leverage is gone.

## The Simp's Delusion: Why Weakness Is a Habit

Weakness isn't genetic. It's learned.

Nice guys believe they must earn approval . Dominant men know they demand it.

### Case Study: The Man Who Stopped Apologizing

"Daniel," a 29-year-old engineer, spent years apologizing for his opinions. He'd qualify every statement with "I think..." or "Maybe..." until his words lost all weight.

Then he learned calibrated dominance:

- "I'm not here to debate. I'm here to lead."

- "You don't get to decide what I feel. I do."

- "If you want a man who pleads for your attention, look elsewhere."

Daniel didn't become "nicer." He became unshakeable.

## How to Dominate Every Interaction: A Step-by-Step Rebellion

1.     Stop Apologizing : Your presence isn't a burden. Your opinions aren't optional.

2.　　Use Silence as a Weapon : Don't fill voids with nervous chatter. Let silence force action.
3.　　Speak in Ultimatums : No ambiguity. No passive language. State your terms.
4.　　Mirror to Disarm, Then Redirect : Build rapport, then shift the narrative to your advantage.
5.　　Weaponize Vulnerability : Don't whine. Don't plead. Frame your past as evidence of strength.
6.　　Demand Reciprocity : Every investment requires return. No free emotional labor.
7.　　Exit Gracefully : If she won't match your energy, walk away. Let her chase you.
8.　　Surround Yourself with Brotherhood : Weak men pull you down. Strong men drag you up.

## The Rebellion: Why Dominance Wins

Dominance isn't about control. It's about clarity .

Nice guys lose because they're indecisive. They're reactive. They let women define the rules of engagement.

Dominant men win because they write their own script . They don't ask permission. They don't seek approval. They don't play games.

Your move :
• Stop begging for attention.
• Stop apologizing for who you are.
• Start leading every conversation.

Dominance isn't a personality trait. It's a tactical skill .

And now, you've got the tools.

# CHAPTER 12: STRATEGIC ABUNDANCE – HOW TO WIN THE DATING GAME (WITHOUT SELLING YOUR SOUL)

You've been told the dating game is fair. That if you "put yourself out there," kindness, patience, and persistence will win you love. But the truth is brutal: the dating market isn't a meritocracy—it's an economy . And in this economy, men are the currency. Women are the investors. And most men are trading at a loss.

Dating apps aren't platforms for connection. They're marketplaces where attention is the commodity . Women hold the monopoly—they receive 70% more matches, 50% more messages, and control the terms of engagement. Men scramble for scraps, offering endless emotional labor, financial investment, and compliance in exchange for a shot at approval.

But here's the reality: you're not broke because you're weak. You're broke because you're bad at economics.

Strategic abundance isn't about playing the game "better." It's about rejecting the game entirely and reclaiming your value . It's about understanding that your attention, time, and emotional energy are finite resources—and treating them like the assets they are.

This chapter arms you with a decision algorithm for the dating economy: when to invest, when to pivot, and when to walk away. No more desperation. No more begging. No more selling your soul for a chance at validation.

## The Dating Economy: Why Men Are the Product, Not the Buyer

Dating apps replicate the worst aspects of capitalism: asymmetry, exploitation, and winner-takes-all dynamics . Here's how the system rigs against men:

• Women receive 2–3x more matches than men , even when controlling for attractiveness (OkCupid, 2022).

• Men send 70% more messages but get fewer responses, creating a cycle of effort and rejection (Hinge, 2023).

• Hypergamy dominates : women prioritize men who offer dominance, status, or genetic upgrades—even in "egalitarian" relationships (Journal of Personality and Social Psychology, 2021).

In this economy, men are the product. Women are the consumers. And like any good marketer, women skim the top —ignoring the "average" guy to chase the 20% of men who embody dominance, confidence, and unavailability.

The Simp's Delusion:

Simps believe they can "earn" attention through effort. They send endless messages, pay for dates, and offer free emotional labor, hoping to out-work the competition. But effort doesn't scale. Value does.

Dominant men understand the rules:

- Don't compete—command.

- Don't give—trade.

- Don't beg—negotiate.

## The Productivity Principle: Why Value Creation Beats Transactional Desperation

Most men treat dating like a job interview:

- They optimize their profiles for approval.

- They tailor their messages to women's preferences.

- They work harder, longer, and more desperately to earn a "job" as a boyfriend.

This is transactional desperation —a losing strategy where men sell their attention cheaply, only to get discarded when a "better deal" comes along.

The alternative? Value creation.

Value creators don't cater to demand. They build their own market . They focus on:

- Becoming desirable (skills, presence, ambition) rather than appeasing women.

- Creating leverage (multiple connections, self-sufficiency) rather than clinging to one woman.

- Demanding reciprocity (effort, loyalty, respect) rather than giving freely.

**Case Study: The Man Who Stopped Applying for Approval**

"James," a 30-year-old designer, spent years chasing women on dating apps. He crafted witty bios, sent personalized messages, and paid for premium subscriptions. He got matches. He got conversations. He got ghosted.

Then he flipped the script.

- He deleted his apps.

- He built his life around value creation : Brazilian jiu-jitsu, entrepreneurship, and brotherhood.

- He rejoined the game with a new rule: *"No free emotional labor. No one-sided investments."*

Suddenly, women chased him. Not because he became "nicer." Because he became unavailable.

## The Decision Algorithm: When to Invest, Pivot, or Disengage

Winning the dating economy requires strategic abundance — a mindset where you operate from surplus, not scarcity. Here's how to assess every interaction through an economic lens:

### Step 1: The Initial Investment – Does She Signal Reciprocity?

Every relationship starts with an investment test:

- Does she respond quickly, or make you wait?

- Does she ask about your life, or treat you like a sounding board?

- Does she invest effort, or expect you to do all the work?

Investment Rule :
- If she reciprocates within 48 hours, proceed.
- If she withholds effort, disappear.

### Case Study: The Ghosting Trap

"Ethan," a 28-year-old engineer, messaged a woman who hadn't replied in three days. She finally responded: *"I've been busy. Are you still interested?"*

Ethan's move?

- He replied: *"I'm not in the business of chasing. If you want to talk, let's talk now. If not, we're done."*

- She didn't text back. Good. Ethan saved himself 20 hours of wasted effort.

Why It Works :

- Scarcity creates value. Ghosting is a signal: she's not invested.

- Walking away forces her to reassess. If you're always available, you're always replaceable.

## Step 2: The Reciprocity Check – Is This a One-Sided Market?

Once she engages, watch for reciprocity:

- Does she ask about your life, or focus only on herself?

- Does she invest in plans, or keep things vague?

- Does she match your effort, or expect you to carry the relationship?

Pivot Rule :

- If she fails the reciprocity check three times, walk away.

### Case Study: The Emotional Labor Trap

"Daniel," a 31-year-old teacher, spent six months listening to a woman vent about her exes, her job, and her "emotional struggles." He offered advice, reassurance, and free therapy.

She never initiated a date. Never asked about his life. Never thanked him.

Daniel's move?

- He stopped responding.

- When she messaged again, he said: *"I'm not your therapist. If you want a real relationship, show up. If not, I'll find someone who will."*

Why It Works :

- Emotional labor is a trap. Women who extract effort without reciprocating are opportunists, not partners.

- Forcing reciprocity filters out users. If she won't invest, she doesn't deserve your time.

## Step 3: The Abundance Exit – When to Walk Away and Reset

Abundance means never relying on one person . If a woman doesn't match your energy, pivot.

Disengagement Rule:

If she:

- Fails the reciprocity check

- Refuses to invest effort

- Ghosting, stonewalling, or gaslighting

Then:

- Delete. Block. Replace.

### Case Study: The Man Who Left the Market

"Chris," a 34-year-old construction worker, spent two years dating women who treated him like a backup plan. He'd pay for dates, listen to complaints, and tolerate emotional games.

Then he quit.

- He sold his dating app subscription.

- He focused on physical training and skill mastery.

- Six months later, women started approaching him.

Why It Works :

- Scarcity creates demand . When you stop chasing, you become the chaser.

- Abundance breaks dependence . If you're not emotionally invested, you can't be manipulated.

## The Simp's Delusion: Why Transactional Desperation Fails

Simps believe they can earn loyalty through effort. They send thoughtful messages, pay for dates, and suppress their needs to avoid conflict. But transactional desperation is a death sentence.

Why Simp Strategies Fail :

- Women exploit effort : The more you give, the more they expect.

- Dominance wins : Women pursue men who appear indifferent, not those who beg.

- Market saturation kills value : If you're always available, you're always replaceable.

### Case Study: The Man Who Sold Himself Short

"Mark," a 29-year-old accountant, dated a woman who demanded constant validation. He texted daily. He paid for dinners. He tolerated her emotional games.

When she broke up with him, she said: *"I just don't feel a spark."*

Mark's mistake wasn't effort. It was free labor.

The Fix :

- Stop giving until she gives back.
- Demand reciprocity before commitment.
- Exit early if she refuses to match your energy.

## The Abundance Mindset: Why Dominance Is the Ultimate Currency

Dominance isn't aggression. It's economic positioning .

Dominant men don't seek approval. They create leverage . They have:

- Multiple connections : They don't need any one woman.
- High-value habits : They build skills, strength, and purpose outside dating.
- Unapologetic boundaries : They don't tolerate disrespect.

The Abundance Algorithm :
1. Assess reciprocity : Does she match your effort?
2. Measure value : Does this interaction make you stronger?
3. Exit if she fails the test : No free labor. No emotional extraction.

Dominant men operate from power , not neediness. They know:

- Attention is a currency .
- Respect must be earned .
- Loyalty is a privilege —not a reward for compliance.

## The Market Exploits Weakness – Here's How to Flip the Script

Dating apps weaponize male desperation. Here's how they do it:

- Endless choice traps: Women scroll indefinitely, always seeking a "better deal."

- Variable rewards: Ghosting keeps men addicted to intermittent validation.
- Emotional extraction: Women extract effort without offering return investment.

Your Move :

- Opt out of the market . Build real connections through shared interests, physical training, or skill-based communities.
- Create value through dominance : Competence, confidence, and unavailability make you irresistible.
- Demand reciprocity : No free labor. No one-sided investments.

**Case Study: The Man Who Reclaimed His Power**
"Ryan," a 27-year-old mechanic, used to spend weekends swiping. He got matches. He got ghosted. He got used.

Then he joined a Brazilian jiu-jitsu gym. Built a side business. Quit dating apps for three months.

When he returned, women pursued him. Not because he changed. Because he stopped playing by their rules.

# The Simp's Downfall: Why Free Labor Gets You Ghosted

Simps believe effort earns loyalty. Evolutionary psychology proves otherwise:

- Women evolved to seek dominance, not compliance.
- Dominant men command loyalty. Simps beg for it.
- Free labor signals weakness. Women subconsciously reject men who give without limits.

**Case Study: The Man Who Paid for His Own Obsolescence**
"Ethan," a 33-year-old engineer, paid for every date. He listened to her problems. He never set boundaries.

When she broke up with him, she said: *"You're a great guy. I just don't get excited by you."*

Ethan's mistake wasn't generosity. It was free labor.

The Fix :
- Demand reciprocity before investment.
- Build value through competence, not compliance.
- Exit early if she refuses to match your energy.

## The Power Move: How to Exit the Game Without Losing

Dominant men don't "lose" in dating. They exit gracefully and come back stronger.

Case Study: The Man Who Refused to Negotiate
"David," a 35-year-old veteran, dated a woman who refused to commit. He paid for dinners. He listened to her complaints. She kept him on a string.

His move?
- He stopped messaging.
- He doubled down on physical training and mentorship.
- Six weeks later, she texted: *"Are you dating anyone?"*
- His reply: *"I'm not in the market. If you're serious, we start fresh. If not, I'll find someone who is."*

Why It Works :
- Silence forces action .
- Dominance creates demand .
- Abundance makes you untouchable .

## How to Win the Game: A Step-by-Step Rebellion

1. Treat Attention as Currency
- No free emotional labor.

- No one-sided investments.
- Demand reciprocity before commitment.

2. Create Leverage Through Abundance
- Build multiple connections.
- Focus on skill mastery, physical training, and brotherhood.
- Stop relying on dating apps to validate your worth.

3. Use Silence as a Weapon
- Ghosters lose power when you refuse to chase.
- Women fear irrelevance. Use it.

4. Demand Reciprocity Before Commitment
- No free labor.
- No one-sided investments.
- No compliance in exchange for crumbs.

5. Exit Early and Exit Clean
- Don't tolerate disrespect.
- Don't beg for closure.
- Disappear. Rebuild. Return with power.

6. Surround Yourself with Brotherhood
- Weak men pull you down.
- Strong men drag you up.
- Build a tribe of warriors, not simps.

7. Reframe Dating as a Marketplace
- You're not a buyer. You're a seller.
- Your value isn't determined by her opinion.
- You set the price. If she won't pay, find someone who will.

## The Rebellion: Why Abundance Beats Desperation

Desperation is a trap. Abundance is a weapon.

Nice guys play the game. Alphas rewrite the rules.

You're not broken. You're not undesirable. You're just playing by a rigged script.

Your move :
- Stop giving freely .
- Demand reciprocity .
- Exit losers early.
- Build value through dominance.

The dating economy wants you broke. Don't let it win.

# CHAPTER 13: BROTHERHOOD AND COMMUNITY – WHY MEN NEED TO STOP RELYING ON WOMEN

You've been taught that women are your source of validation. That your worth is measured by their attention, their affection, their loyalty. You've spent your life chasing approval from women—texting first, paying for dates, tolerating disrespect, and suppressing your needs to avoid conflict. And what did it get you? Ghosting. Betrayal. A lifetime of feeling invisible.

Here's the truth: women are not your tribe.

Evolution built men to bond with other men. To fight together, hunt together, build together. Brotherhood was the foundation of survival. Without it, men became isolated, weak, and vulnerable. Today, male friendship networks have collapsed. The Pew Research Center reports that 50% of men have no close male friends , compared to 20% of women. Men are lonelier than ever. More depressed. More likely to die from "deaths of despair" (suicide, drug overdose, alcoholism).

This isn't an accident. It's a system failure.

Feminism dismantled male bonding under the guise of "toxic

masculinity." Corporate culture replaced mentorship with HR sensitivity training. Social media turned men into isolated consumers, scrolling alone instead of training, building, or fighting together. And dating apps weaponized this isolation, making men desperate for female validation because they have no one else.

But here's the solution: brotherhood is armor.

Structured rituals—physical training, skill mastery, service to a cause—create the kind of bonds that once defined masculinity. These aren't therapy circles or "emotional check-ins." They're tactical units, designed to rebuild the warrior ethos that made men indispensable.

## The Simp's Trap: Why Female Dependency Destroys Men

Dependency isn't love. It's submission.

Men who rely on women for validation become emotionally fragile, desperate for approval, and easy to discard. They tolerate disrespect. They apologize for their existence. They bend over backwards to earn scraps of affection.

### Case Study: The Man Who Gave Everything
"James," a 29-year-old teacher, spent years dating women who treated him like a backup plan. He paid for dinners, listened to their problems, and suppressed his needs to avoid conflict. When they ghosted him, he spiraled into depression.

James's mistake? He outsourced his tribal identity to women. Without male friends, without brotherhood, he had no one to remind him that his value wasn't tied to a woman's opinion.

Data Point :
•    Men with fewer than three close male friends are 3x more likely to experience suicidal ideation than men with strong

brotherhood networks (CDC, 2023).

* Men who rely on romantic relationships for self-worth are 50% more likely to stay in abusive or one-sided partnerships (Journal of Abnormal Psychology, 2022).

Dependency isn't weakness. It's programming —a product of a culture that stripped men of their natural alliances and sold them the lie that women are their only source of meaning.

## The Warrior's Blueprint: Why Brotherhood Is Biological Imperative

Evolution didn't design men to live alone. We were built for tribes. For packs. For brotherhood.

Anthropologist Robert Sapolsky's fieldwork with baboon troops revealed a universal truth: men thrive in structured male communities. In troops where older males trained younger ones in dominance, hierarchy, and cooperation, younger males grew into leaders. In tribes where men trained together, fought together, and built together, men felt purpose.

Today, that purpose is gone.

### Case Study: The Man Who Found His Tribe

"Daniel," a 34-year-old mechanic, spent his 20s isolated. He dated women who used him for emotional labor, paid for dinners he couldn't afford, and felt invisible when they ghosted him. Then he joined a Brazilian jiu-jitsu gym.

Suddenly, he had a new identity : a fighter, a student, a leader. Women started chasing him—not because he changed his behavior, but because he stopped needing them to feel whole.

Daniel didn't become "nicer." He became unavailable.

## Structured Rituals: The Weaponization of Brotherhood

Brotherhood isn't about "vibes" or casual hangouts. It's about rituals that build dominance, loyalty, and unshakable self-respect.

Here are the three pillars of structured male bonding:

**1. Physical Training Cohorts – The Return of the Warrior Class**
Physical training isn't just for aesthetics. It's a rite of passage.

Martial arts, weightlifting, obstacle-course training—these aren't hobbies. They're tribal initiation rituals . They teach men to endure, to fight, to lead. More importantly, they forge bonds through shared struggle.

Why It Works:

- Testosterone and camaraderie: Physical exertion spikes testosterone, which fuels dominance and confidence.
- Dominance hierarchies: Men naturally form hierarchies in training environments. Respect is earned, not given.
- Resilience under pressure: Training teaches men to push through pain, a skill that translates directly to relationships.

**Case Study: The Gym That Built More Than Muscles**
"Mark," a 31-year-old accountant, joined a CrossFit gym after years of failed relationships. He learned to lift weights, compete, and train with other men.

Within six months, his confidence skyrocketed. He stopped chasing women. He stopped tolerating disrespect. Women started pursuing him. Not because he changed his personality—but because he stopped needing them to validate his strength.

Your Move :

- Find a physical training group (judo, boxing, weightlifting, parkour).
- Train with men who demand excellence —not "supportive" simps.
- Treat every session as a war game : build endurance, test

limits, dominate.

## 2. Skill Guilds – The Death of the "Just a Guy" Mentality
Men without skills are men without purpose.

In ancestral environments, men bonded over craft, strategy, and mastery. Hunters learned from elders. Warriors trained together. Builders collaborated on survival. Today, men are told to "share feelings" in therapy circles or "network" at corporate mixers. Weakness dressed as progress.

Why It Fails :
- Emotional vulnerability without dominance is submission .
- Networking events are transactional —no loyalty, no shared struggle.
- Skill mastery builds real status —the kind that attracts women without begging for it.

Skill Guilds as Tactical Brotherhood :
- Apprenticeship models: Learn from men who've already won—craftsmen, veterans, mentors.
- Competitive skill-building: Build a craft (woodworking, coding, leadership) and use it to command respect.
- Guilds over networking: Join or create groups where men trade knowledge, strategy, and loyalty.

### Case Study: The Man Who Built His Own Value
"Ethan," a 28-year-old software developer, spent years chasing women who treated him like a backup plan. Then he joined a coding guild—a group of men who shared projects, critiqued each other's work, and competed to build better products.

Within a year, Ethan's confidence exploded. He stopped tolerating women who demanded free emotional labor. He started dating women who respected him. Not because he "improved." Because he stopped needing approval.

Your Move :
- Pick a skill and dominate it: coding, combat, craftsmanship.
- Join or build a guild: a group of men who train, compete, and grow together.
- Treat skill mastery as dominance: your value isn't tied to a woman's opinion—it's tied to your ability to win.

**3. Service Projects – The Antidote to Emotional Desperation**
Men need a cause bigger than themselves.

Feminism and digital culture sell the lie that service is about "giving back" or "emotional labor." Wrong. Service is about proving your worth through action. It's what made soldiers follow generals. It's what made hunters fight for their tribe.

Why Service Builds Brotherhood :
- Shared purpose: Fighting for something bigger than yourself creates unbreakable bonds.
- Action over talk: Brotherhood isn't built in therapy circles. It's built through mission-driven action.
- Status through sacrifice: Men who serve a cause earn respect —not through words, but through evidence of loyalty.

**Case Study: The Man Who Found His Mission**
"Chris," a 36-year-old veteran, returned from deployment feeling hollow. He spent years chasing women who treated him like a disposable asset. Then he joined a mentorship program for at-risk youth.

Suddenly, he had a new identity: protector, leader, mentor. Women noticed. Not because Chris changed his personality— but because he stopped needing their approval to feel whole.

Your Move :
- Serve a cause that demands loyalty : mentoring, military service, community rebuilding.

- Build brotherhood through mission : men who fight together don't need women to define their worth.
- Let your actions speak : strength isn't in words. It's in what you do.

## The Simp's Delusion: Why Female Validation Is a Trap

Simps believe women are the source of their worth. Evolutionary psychology says otherwise.

Primate studies show that dominant males receive mating access because they lead their tribe , not because they beg for female approval. Human societies mirror this dynamic. Men who lead, build, and fight together attract loyalty—from women, from employers, from peers. Men who chase women like simps get discarded like disposable assets.

### Case Study: The Man Who Refused to Be Used

"Ryan," a 30-year-old sales rep, spent years dating women who treated him like a sounding board. He gave endlessly, got nothing back. Then he joined a volunteer fire department.

Suddenly, he had a new identity: protector. He stopped texting women who ghosted him. He stopped apologizing for who he was. Women started chasing him. Not because he became "nicer." Because he stopped needing them to define his worth.

Why It Works :

- Women want men with purpose —not men who exist to please them.
- Brotherhood builds dominance : men who fight together don't need women to validate their strength.
- Service creates loyalty : men who serve a cause become indispensable.

## The Modern Tribe: How to Rebuild Brotherhood in a

## World That Hates Men

Brotherhood isn't about "toxic masculinity." It's about reclaiming what feminism stole: the right to bond, to lead, to dominate.

Here's how to start:

1. Find the Right Tribe
- Avoid "men's circles" that teach you to cry into a journal. Look for groups that demand action, skill, and loyalty.
- Join martial arts gyms, tactical training programs, or apprenticeships where men earn respect through dominance.

2. Build Your Own Guild
- Find 3–5 men who share your values.
- Create a ritual: weekly training, skill-sharing, accountability.
- Demand loyalty. If someone betrays the code, remove them.

3. Serve a Cause Bigger Than Yourself
- Mentor younger men. Fight for your community. Build something that lasts.
- Let your actions prove your worth.

4. Reject Weakness
- Weak men pull you down. Strong men drag you up.
- If a man talks about "feelings" instead of action, cut him loose.

5. Use Brotherhood as a Weapon
- Women don't respect men who need them. They respect men who have something to lose .
- Brotherhood gives you leverage.

## The Warrior's Code: Why Brotherhood Destroys

## Female Dependency

Dependency is a mindset. Brotherhood is a tactical shift .

When you build bonds with men, you stop seeing women as the center of your world. You stop tolerating disrespect. You stop begging for approval. You become unfuckwithable .

Case Study: The Man Who Stopped Needing Approval
"David," a 33-year-old construction worker, spent his 20s chasing women who treated him like a backup plan. He apologized for his opinions, tolerated emotional labor, and got discarded like a disposable asset.

Then he joined a tactical shooting group. He learned to lead. To protect. To fight. Suddenly, women chased him. Not because he changed. Because he stopped needing them to feel whole.

Why It Works :
- Loyalty is earned through action .
- Strength is proven through dominance .
- Purpose isn't found in women —it's forged in battle.

## The Simp's Downfall: Why Isolation Makes You Disposable

Weak men isolate. Strong men build tribes .

Isolation breeds desperation. Desperation leads to compliance. Compliance gets you ghosted.

Data Point :
- Men who lack male friends are twice as likely to accept one-sided relationships where they give everything and get nothing (Pew Research, 2023).
- Men who train with other men are 3x more likely to attract partners who respect them (Personality and Social Psychology Review, 2021).

**Case Study: The Man Who Broke the Cycle**
"Jason," a 35-year-old mechanic, spent his 20s in relationships where he was used and discarded. He had no male friends. No mentors. No tribe.

Then he joined a motorcycle club. He learned to ride, repair engines, and lead rides. He stopped dating women who disrespected him. Within a year, women chased him. Not because he became "better." Because he stopped needing their approval.

Why It Works:
- Brotherhood builds dominance.
- Shared struggle builds loyalty.
- Men who belong to a tribe don't beg for scraps.

# How to Build Brotherhood: A Step-by-Step Rebellion

1. Identify Your Tribe
- Find men who dominate, not men who complain.
- Train with warriors, not simps.

2. Create a Ritual
- Weekly training sessions.
- Skill-sharing workshops.
- Mentorship programs for younger men.

3. Build a Hierarchy
- Respect is earned, not given.
- Demand effort. Reward dominance.

4. Fight for a Cause
- Mentor at-risk youth. Volunteer in your community. Serve a mission.
- Let your actions prove your worth.

5. Reject Weakness

- Cut men who drain your energy.
- Surround yourself with warriors.

  6. Let Brotherhood Be Your Armor
- Women will respect you when you stop needing their approval.
- Brotherhood builds dominance.

  7. Use Brotherhood as Leverage
- Women pursue men who have something to lose.
- Brotherhood gives you that something.

## The Rebellion: Why Brotherhood Is the Ultimate Weapon

Brotherhood isn't about "friendship." It's about dominance.

Men who train together, build together, and fight together don't need women to define their worth . They don't tolerate disrespect. They don't beg for approval. They command it.

Nice guys isolate. Alphas build tribes.

Your Move:

- Stop chasing women who use you.

- Start building a tribe that demands your loyalty.

- Let brotherhood be your armor.

The next chapter shows you how to define your own masculine ethos—strength, empathy, resilience, and purpose. But first, remember:

You were never meant to survive alone.

You were built to dominate with brothers beside you.

# CHAPTER 14: A NEW MASCULINE ETHOS – WHY STRENGTH, EMPATHY, AND PURPOSE MATTER NOW MORE THAN EVER

You've been told masculinity is obsolete. That strength is toxic. That empathy is weakness. That resilience is "grinding" for a system that exploits you. That purpose is a fantasy sold by self-help gurus who want your money.

Here's the truth: masculinity isn't dead. It's been weaponized against you.

The old rules—provision, protection, dominance—weren't flawed. They were hijacked by a culture that wanted men docile, dependent, and disposable. Feminism stripped men of their roles, then mocked them for feeling lost. Corporations turned men into replaceable assets, then gaslit them into believing emotional vulnerability would fix everything. And dating apps reduced masculinity to a commodity, where men compete for scraps of female approval.

But strength, empathy, resilience, and purpose aren't relics of a dying world. They're the blueprint for rebellion.

This chapter defines a new masculine ethos—one that rejects weakness, rejects compliance, and rejects the lie that men must apologize for who they are. These four pillars aren't abstract ideals. They're tactical advantages , tools to dominate the modern world while staying true to your evolutionary design.

## Strength: The Reliable Application of Power for the Benefit of Self and Others

Strength isn't brute force. It's dominance made actionable.

Evolution built men to apply power—physically, socially, and emotionally. But modern culture has twisted strength into submission. Men are told to "tone it down," "play nice," and "share feelings" in therapy circles. Weakness disguised as progress.

Real strength isn't aggression. It's the ability to act decisively, lead with authority, and protect what's yours. It's the warrior who defends his tribe. The leader who commands respect. The father who provides without apology.

### Case Study: The Man Who Stopped Apologizing

"Daniel," a 32-year-old mechanic, spent years apologizing for his presence. He softened his voice, avoided confrontation, and let women walk all over him. Then he joined a Brazilian jiu-jitsu gym.

Suddenly, he had a new identity: a fighter. He learned to apply power with precision—on the mat and off it. Women stopped testing him. Employers respected his discipline. Even his father —who'd always criticized him—asked for advice.

Daniel didn't become "nicer." He became unfuckwithable.

Why It Works:

- Strength isn't about violence—it's about control.

- Dominance isn't earned through compliance—it's commanded through action.

- Men who apply power reliably earn loyalty, respect, and fear.

Your Move:

- Train your body: Build physical strength through martial arts, weightlifting, or tactical training.

- Lead in every room: Speak with clarity, take charge of conversations, and refuse to be sidelined.

- Protect what's yours: Set boundaries and enforce them without apology.

## Empathy: Disciplined Perspective-Taking, Not Emotional Submission

Empathy isn't about crying into a journal. It's about reading people like a battlefield.

Weak men believe empathy means agreeing with women, tolerating disrespect, and offering free emotional labor. Strong men know empathy is a strategic tool —a way to decode others' motivations, anticipate manipulation, and navigate social dynamics with precision.

Why Empathy Isn't Weakness:

- Dominant men use empathy to control : They read emotions, predict behavior, and steer interactions.

- Empathy without dominance is submission : Listening without leverage makes you a pawn.

- Perspective-taking builds influence : Knowing what others want lets you negotiate from power.

**Case Study: The Man Who Outmaneuvered the Game**
"Ethan," a 30-year-old engineer, used to get ghosted constantly. He'd listen to women's problems, validate their feelings, and apologize for his own needs. Then he started studying human behavior.

He learned to read micro-expressions, decode subtext, and respond with calibrated vulnerability. Suddenly, women stopped ghosting him. They started chasing him. Not because Ethan became "nicer"—because he became unpredictable.

Why It Works:

- Empathy is a weapon : It lets you see manipulation before it happens.

- Dominance is earned through insight : Knowing what others want gives you leverage.

- Strength without empathy is blindness : You can't lead if you don't understand the terrain.

Your Move:

- Master micro-expressions : Learn to read body language and tone.

- Use empathy to control : Know what others want before they ask.

- Don't give freely : Empathy without boundaries is exploitation.

## Resilience: Iterative Adaptation to Adversity
Resilience isn't about "grinding harder." It's about learning,

adjusting, and coming back stronger.

Nice guys grind until they break. Alphas adapt. Evolution built men to survive—through trial, error, and relentless iteration. Every setback is a data point. Every failure is a lesson.

Why Resilience Isn't Weakness:

- Resilience is strategic: It's not about enduring pain—it's about learning from it.
- Adaptation wins: Men who pivot after failure outperform those who cling to broken strategies.
- Resilience builds dominance: Men who recover from rejection command respect.

**Case Study: The Man Who Turned Failure into Leverage**
"Chris," a 34-year-old teacher, got rejected by women who wanted more "excitement." He could've wallowed. Instead, he treated rejection like a business report:

- What worked?
- What failed?
- What adjustments needed to be made?

Within six months, Chris had a new strategy. He stopped chasing women who disrespected him. He started dating women who respected his energy. Not because he became "better." Because he became unpredictable.

Why It Works:
- Resilience isn't about endurance—it's about evolution.
- Failure isn't the end—it's a diagnostic tool .
- Dominant men use setbacks to refine their approach.

Your Move:
- Treat rejection as feedback : Adjust your strategy, don't collapse.
- Use failure as fuel : Every setback is a lesson in dominance.

- Build mental armor : Train your brain to see adversity as opportunity.

## Purpose: Devotion to a Cause Larger Than Personal Gain

Purpose isn't about "finding yourself." It's about becoming indispensable.

Feminism sold men the lie that their value comes from women's approval. Corporate culture told them to trade passion for a paycheck. Social media trained them to measure worth in likes and followers. But evolution designed men to fight for something bigger—tribes, missions, causes that demanded loyalty and sacrifice.

Why Purpose Isn't Weakness :

- Purpose builds dominance : Men who serve a cause command respect.
- Loyalty is earned through sacrifice : People follow men who risk everything for a mission.
- Purpose creates leverage : A man with a cause isn't replaceable.

### Case Study: The Man Who Refused to Be Disposable

"Ryan," a 29-year-old mechanic, spent his 20s dating women who treated him like a backup plan. He had no direction. No mission. No leverage. Then he joined a mentorship program for at-risk youth.

Suddenly, he had a new identity: protector, leader, mentor. Women noticed. Not because Ryan changed his personality—but because he stopped needing their approval to feel whole.

Why It Works :

- Women chase men with purpose : A cause proves your value isn't transactional.
- Purpose builds unshakeable self-respect : Your worth isn't

tied to a woman's opinion.
- Loyalty is earned through action : Men who serve a mission attract followers—and partners.

Your Move :
- Find a cause that demands your loyalty : Martial arts, mentorship, community rebuilding.
- Build a legacy : Let your actions prove your worth.
- Let purpose be your filter : If it doesn't serve your mission, it doesn't serve you.

## The Simp's Delusion: Why Weakness Fails

Weak men believe strength is aggression, empathy is compliance, resilience is suffering, and purpose is optional. They apologize for their existence. They tolerate disrespect. They fold under pressure. They drift through life waiting for someone to validate them.

And they get discarded.

Dominant men know the truth:
- Strength isn't aggression—it's control.
- Empathy isn't submission—it's strategy.
- Resilience isn't endurance—it's evolution.
- Purpose isn't optional—it's oxygen.

### Case Study: The Man Who Rewrote His Identity

"Mark," a 33-year-old veteran, returned from deployment feeling invisible. He dated women who treated him like a disposable asset. Then he started training younger men in combat techniques. He led workouts. He mentored. He built a tribe.

Suddenly, women chased him. Not because he changed. Because he stopped needing their approval to feel whole.

Why It Works :

- Dominant men don't seek validation—they demand it .
- Purpose creates leverage : You're not replaceable if you're irreplaceable.
- Strength, empathy, resilience, and purpose form a feedback loop : Each trait reinforces the others.

## The Warrior's Code: Why This Ethos Wins

Strength, empathy, resilience, and purpose aren't abstract ideals. They're tactical advantages.

- Strength lets you command respect.
- Empathy lets you control the narrative.
- Resilience lets you survive setbacks.
- Purpose makes you indispensable.

**Case Study: The Man Who Became Unshakable**

"David," a 35-year-old construction worker, spent his 20s chasing women who treated him like a backup plan. He apologized for his opinions, tolerated emotional games, and felt invisible. Then he rebuilt his life around the four pillars:

- Strength: He trained Brazilian jiu-jitsu.
- Empathy: He learned to read people like a battlefield.
- Resilience: He treated failure as a learning opportunity.
- Purpose: He started mentoring younger men.

Within a year, women started chasing him. Not because he became "better." Because he became unavailable.

Why It Works:

- Dominance isn't inherited—it's built.
- Purpose isn't optional—it's leverage.
- Resilience isn't about endurance—it's about evolution.
- Empathy isn't weakness—it's strategy.

## The New Alpha Ethos: Why This Is Your Ultimate

## Weapon

Nice guys fail because they play by outdated rules. Alphas win because they rewrite the game.

Strength, empathy, resilience, and purpose aren't about being "good." They're about being unassailable.

- Strength ensures you're not a victim.
- Empathy ensures you're not a pawn.
- Resilience ensures you're not disposable.
- Purpose ensures you're not replaceable.

**Case Study: The Man Who Redefined Masculinity**
"James," a 31-year-old accountant, spent his 20s apologizing for who he was. He chased women who ghosted him, tolerated disrespect, and felt invisible. Then he rebuilt his identity around the four pillars:

- Strength : He learned Brazilian jiu-jitsu.
- Empathy : He studied human behavior.
- Resilience : He treated failure as a diagnostic tool.
- Purpose : He started mentoring younger men.

Suddenly, women chased him. Not because he became "nicer." Because he stopped needing their approval to feel whole.

Why It Works :
- Dominance isn't about aggression—it's about control.
- Empathy isn't about submission—it's about strategy.
- Resilience isn't about endurance—it's about adaptation.
- Purpose isn't about charity—it's about leverage.

## The Rebellion: Why This Ethos Is the Future of Masculinity

The old rules are obsolete. But the answer isn't to surrender. It's to reclaim your power .

Strength, empathy, resilience, and purpose aren't about becoming "better." They're about becoming unassailable.

Dominant men don't apologize for who they are. They refuse to be used . They don't chase approval. They command it . They don't tolerate disrespect. They enforce boundaries.

Your Move:
- Strength: Build it through physical training, leadership, and control.
- Empathy: Use it to decode people, not submit to them.
- Resilience: Treat failure as a feedback loop, not a death sentence.
- Purpose: Serve a mission that demands loyalty, not validation.

The rebellion isn't about fighting women. It's about reclaiming your place in the world .

This isn't the end. It's the beginning.

Your move :
- Stop apologizing for who you are.
- Start applying power with precision.
- Build a life that demands loyalty.

The future of masculinity starts here.

# EPILOGUE

*Authorship Over Accident – How
to Write Your Own Rules*

You've been told your life is predetermined.

Your genes wrote your instincts.

Your childhood shaped your fears.

The algorithm dictates your choices.

But here's the truth: you are not a prisoner of accident . You are the author of your story. The opening chapters may have been written by evolution, culture, and trauma—but the rest is yours to edit.

This book has armed you with the tools to reclaim your power:
- Strength to dominate your environment.
- Empathy to decode manipulation.
- Resilience to adapt after setbacks.
- Purpose to anchor your identity beyond romantic validation.

Now, it's time to write your own rules.

## The First Draft: Genes, Algorithms, and Childhood Scripts

Evolution gave you instincts designed for a world of scarcity and status.

- Your aggression was survival.
- Your dominance was necessity.
- Your desire for loyalty was strategy.

But modern culture rewrote your code.
- Algorithms weaponized your dopamine against you.
- Dating apps turned you into a commodity .
- Feminism stripped you of your role —then mocked you for feeling lost.

Your childhood added another layer.
- Attachment wounds taught you to chase approval.
- Cultural narratives told you to apologize for ambition.
- Weakness became your default.

These forces shaped your first draft.

But they don't get to write the ending.

## The Rebellion Begins: Rewriting Your Narrative

A story is not a sentence. It's a series of choices . Every day, every interaction, every decision is a chance to edit the script.

### Case Study: The Man Who Stopped Living by Default

"Mark," a 32-year-old sales rep, spent his 20s chasing women who treated him like a backup plan. He believed his loneliness was fate. Then he realized: he was living by default, not design.

He rewrote his rules:

- No more free emotional labor : He demanded reciprocity.

- No more ghosting : He disappeared from women who disrespected him.

- No more isolation : He built a tribe of warriors, not simps.

Suddenly, women chased him. Not because he changed his

personality—but because he stopped letting others define his worth.

Why It Works:

- Authorship is power : When you stop reacting and start directing, you reclaim control.

- Editing is rebellion : Every rewrite is a rejection of weakness.

- Dominance is a choice : You don't inherit it. You build it.

## Tools for Rebellion: Your Tactical Kit

You don't fight with words alone. You fight with resources — weapons that turn theory into action. Here's your toolkit:

**1. Cognitive-Behavioral Therapy (CBT) – Rewire Your Brain for Dominance**

CBT isn't about "fixing" yourself. It's about hacking your mind to eliminate self-sabotage.

- **Recommended Resources:**

  - *Feeling Good* by David Burns (for practical CBT techniques).

  - Online directories: Psychology Today, Therapist Aid, or BetterHelp (search for therapists specializing in male identity, trauma, or performance psychology).

  - Apps: Moodpath, CBT Companion (for daily habit-building).

How to Use It:

- Identify self-defeating thoughts (*"I'm not good enough"* ).

- Replace them with dominance-driven reframes (*"I command respect"* ).

- Track progress daily. Your brain is a battlefield—make it work for you.

## 2. Evidence-Based Men's Groups – Brotherhood Is Your Armor

Weak men isolate. Strong men build tribes .

- **Recommended Communities:**

    - Physical Training Groups: Brazilian jiu-jitsu gyms, weightlifting crews, parkour collectives.

    - Skill Guilds: Coding guilds, craftsmanship workshops, leadership circles.

    - Mentorship Programs: Outward Bound, tactical training groups, or local volunteer fire departments.

How to Use It:

- Join groups that demand effort, not just "emotional sharing."

- Build loyalty through action, not words.

- Let brotherhood be your shield against female dependency.

## 3. Physical Training – Strength as Your Tactical Edge

Strength isn't vanity. It's leverage .

- **Recommended Programs:**

    - Brazilian jiu-jitsu (for dominance and discipline).

    - Weightlifting (for presence and physical authority).

    - Parkour (for adaptability and mental toughness).

    - Tactical training (for real-world application of power).

How to Use It:

- Train with men who demand excellence, not simps.

- Use physicality to command space—posture, voice, eye contact.

- Let your body prove your dominance before your words ever need to.

## 4. Skill Mastery – Competence as Your Currency

You're not defined by your job title. You're defined by what you build, fix, and create .

- **Recommended Paths:**

  - Martial arts (for presence and discipline).

  - Entrepreneurship (for financial independence).

  - Craftsmanship (for tangible proof of your value).

How to Use It:

- Pick a skill and dominate it.

- Let competence replace compliance as your identity.

- Build leverage through mastery—women chase men who win.

## 5. Service Projects – Purpose as Your Filter

A cause bigger than yourself proves your worth isn't transactional.

- **Recommended Causes:**

  - Mentorship programs (for at-risk youth).

- Community rebuilding (for tangible impact).

- Tactical volunteering (firefighting, emergency response).

How to Use It:

- Serve with loyalty, not guilt.

- Let purpose be your filter: if it doesn't serve your mission, it doesn't serve you.

- Build unshakable self-respect through action, not approval.

## The Simp's Downfall: Why Default Is a Death Sentence

Simps live by accident. They react to women's texts. They follow dating app algorithms. They apologize for who they are.

Dominant men live by design. They set boundaries. They build value. They refuse to be used.

**Case Study: The Man Who Stopped Letting Life Happen to Him**
"James," a 30-year-old engineer, spent years dating women who treated him like a disposable asset. He followed their rules, tolerated disrespect, and felt invisible.

Then he started writing his own script:
- He joined a Brazilian jiu-jitsu gym.
- He quit dating apps for three months.
- He built a side business to prove his value outside romance.

When he returned, women chased him. Not because he changed. Because he stopped letting others define him.

Why It Works :
- Default mode gets you ghosted.
- Authorship gets you respected.
- Rebellion gets you remembered.

## The Warrior's Code: Why You Must Keep Editing

Your story isn't static. It's a living document .

Every setback is a chance to revise. Every rejection is a data point. Every failure is a lesson in dominance.

**Case Study: The Man Who Refused to Settle**
"Ethan," a 29-year-old mechanic, spent his 20s dating women who treated him like a backup plan. He believed his loneliness was fate.

Then he became his own editor:

- He rewrote his rules: *"No free emotional labor. No one-sided investments."*
- He rebuilt his habits: *"Train first. Women second."*
- He reframed his narrative: *"My value isn't tied to approval."*

Suddenly, women started chasing him. Not because he became "nicer." Because he became unavailable.

Why It Works :

- Editing isn't weakness—it's strategy.
- Revising isn't surrender—it's dominance.
- Rewriting isn't compromise—it's war.

## The Final Move: How to Live as the Author of Your Life

Dominant men don't wait for permission. They take control .

Here's how to close the loop:

1. Audit Your Story:
- What rules did you inherit?
- What habits serve weakness?
- What beliefs keep you stuck?

2. Reclaim Your Agency:
- Delete dating apps that commodify your value.
- Replace people-pleasing with dominance.
- Trade compliance for calibrated vulnerability.

3. Build Your Tribe:
- Find men who demand excellence.
- Train, build, and fight with them.
- Reject weakness in all its forms.

4. Serve a Mission:
- Pick a cause that demands loyalty.
- Let purpose be your filter.
- Build a legacy that outlasts romantic validation.

5. Iterate Relentlessly:
- Every failure is a lesson.
- Every setback is a revision.
- Every ghosting is a signal: *"They weren't worthy of your story."*

6. Reject Weakness:
- Cut men who drain your energy.
- Walk away from women who test your limits.
- Disappear from conversations that demand apology.

7. Live by Your Code:
- Define your non-negotiables.
- Enforce them ruthlessly.
- Let your actions speak louder than your words.

## Your Move

You are not broken.
You are not obsolete.
You are not a victim of culture, biology, or betrayal.

You are the author.
The pen is in your hand.
The page is blank.
Write your own damn rules.

Recommended Resources for Rebellion

- Books: *The 48 Laws of Power* (Robert Greene), *Man's Search for Meaning* (Viktor Frankl), *Tribe* (Sebastian Junger).
- Podcasts: *The Art of Manliness* , *Mark Manson's Podcast* , *The Model Health Show* .
- Therapy: Psychology Today, BetterHelp (filter for male-focused or CBT-trained therapists).
- Men's Groups: Brotherhood gyms, skill guilds, mentorship programs.
- Physical Training: Brazilian jiu-jitsu, weightlifting, parkour.

Your Move :
- Delete dating apps.
- Join a gym.
- Start writing.

The rebellion starts now.

Your story isn't over.

It's just getting started.

# GLOSSARY OF TERMS AND CONCEPTS
*(Alphabetical Order)*

**Altruistic Punishment**
Definition : The tendency to punish unfair behavior, even at personal cost, to reinforce social norms.
Context : In modern relationships, men often tolerate disrespect or imbalance because they fear being labeled "toxic" for asserting boundaries.
Relevance : Dominant men use altruistic punishment strategically—refusing to tolerate exploitation while maintaining self-respect. Weak men use it reactively, fueling resentment.

**Attachment Styles**
Definition : Patterns of emotional bonding formed in early childhood, categorized as secure , anxious , or avoidant .
Context : Anxious attachment leads to desperate efforts to secure approval; avoidant attachment fosters emotional withdrawal. Both sabotage relationships by creating imbalance.
Relevance : Dominant men cultivate earned security —a self-built sense of emotional stability that rejects manipulation.

**Beta Male**
Definition : A man who suppresses dominance, prioritizes compliance, and seeks validation through effort rather than presence.

Context : Beta males dominate modern mating markets as low-investment partners who offer emotional labor, financial support, or unconditional loyalty.

Relevance : The book reframes beta behavior as a choice , not a fate, showing how neuroplasticity and strategic abundance can transform beta males into alphas.

## Brotherhood

Definition : Structured male communities built around shared struggle, skill mastery, and mutual loyalty.

Context : Weak men isolate; strong men build brotherhoods through physical training, mentorship, or mission-driven service.

Relevance : Brotherhood acts as armor against female dependency , providing identity, purpose, and resilience.

## Covert Contracts

Definition : Unspoken agreements where men assume effort will earn loyalty (e.g., "If I pay for dates, she'll commit").

Context : Women rarely honor covert contracts because they're unspoken. Simps believe effort guarantees reward; alphas demand reciprocity.

Relevance : The book urges men to replace covert contracts with explicit expectations to avoid exploitation.

## Dating Economy

Definition : The marketplace of romantic attention where women hold disproportionate power and men compete for scraps.

Context : Dating apps reward dominance, confidence, and unavailability while punishing compliance.

Relevance : Men must reject transactional desperation and adopt strategic abundance —building value outside the dating market to reclaim leverage.

**Death of Despair**
Definition : Mortality linked to hopelessness, often tied to economic decline, social isolation, and loss of purpose.
Context : Men are disproportionately affected by deaths of despair (suicide, drug overdose, alcoholism) due to declining male roles.
Relevance : Brotherhood, physical training, and purpose-based living combat despair by rebuilding masculine identity.

**Dominance**
Definition : The ability to command respect through presence, competence, and unshakable self-respect.
Context : Dominance isn't aggression; it's controlled strength that signals value and deters exploitation.
Relevance : Dominance replaces people-pleasing, allowing men to set boundaries and attract loyalty without begging.

**Emotional Labor**
Definition : Unpaid emotional work (listening, problem-solving, validation) disproportionately shouldered by men in modern relationships.
Context : Women often extract emotional labor without reciprocation, creating one-sided dynamics.
Relevance : The book frames emotional labor as a trap —men must demand reciprocity or walk away.

**Emotional Self-Regulation**
Definition : The ability to manage emotional responses through deliberate practice and discipline.
Context : Anxiously attached men struggle with regulation, leading to desperation; avoidant men suppress emotions, leading to disconnection.
Relevance : Neuroplasticity allows men to rewire emotional responses, replacing panic with control.

**Evolutionary Lag**
Definition : Mismatch between ancestral instincts and modern realities (e.g., hypergamy in a world of female financial independence).
Context : Evolution built women to seek status and dominance; modern feminism dismantled male pathways to those traits.
Relevance : Evolutionary lag explains why compliance fails— men must adapt instincts through skill mastery and strategic abundance.

**Ghosting**
Definition : Sudden, unexplained disappearance from a relationship or communication.
Context : Women use ghosting to test men's desperation; men use it to regain power by refusing to engage with disrespect.
Relevance : Ghosting becomes a weapon when used tactically , not reactively.

**Hypergamy**
Definition : The instinctive female drive to seek partners who elevate social or genetic status.
Context : Hypergamy explains why women prefer dominant men, even in egalitarian societies.
Relevance : Men must reject compliance and cultivate dominance to compete in a hypergamous world.

**Mate Guarding**
Definition : Behaviors that protect romantic investments (e.g., vigilance, commitment demands).
Context : Women historically relied on mate guarding to secure resources; men now need it to avoid being replaced by higher-status rivals.
Relevance : Strategic abundance reduces the need for mate guarding by making men unreplaceable through value creation.

**Mate Value**
Definition : A person's desirability based on evolved preferences (e.g., status, ambition, physical presence).
Context : Mate value isn't fixed; it's built through competence, confidence, and purpose.
Relevance : Men must increase mate value through skill mastery and unavailability, not compliance.

**Neuroplasticity**
Definition : The brain's ability to rewire itself through deliberate practice and environmental modeling.
Context : Men can override evolutionary programming (e.g., anxiety, avoidant behavior) through structured training and therapy.
Relevance : Neuroplasticity is the foundation for weaponized masculinity —rewiring weakness into dominance.

**Nonviolent Communication (NVC)**
Definition : A framework for resolving conflict through observation, feeling, need, and request.
Context : Simps misuse NVC to apologize for their existence; alphas weaponize it to set boundaries.
Relevance : The book teaches how to use NVC for tactical clarity , not submission.

**Omega Male**
Definition : A man who fully disengages from mating markets, often in rejection of rigged systems.
Context : Omegas reject competition but lose leverage; dominant men reject exploitation while remaining engaged on their own terms.
Relevance : The book encourages rebellion, not resignation— omega energy is a trap , not a solution.

**Parental Investment Theory**
Definition : Evolutionary principle stating that the sex investing more in offspring (females) becomes selective, while the less-investing sex (males) competes.
Context : Feminism disrupted this dynamic by granting women financial independence but offering men no new path to respect.
Relevance : Men must reclaim investment value through competence, dominance, and purpose.


**People-Pleasing**
Definition : Suppressing needs to avoid conflict or gain approval, often leading to resentment.
Context : Nice guys use people-pleasing to earn loyalty; women exploit it by demanding more effort.
Relevance : The book frames people-pleasing as submission , not virtue, urging men to demand reciprocity.


**Reciprocity**
Definition : The mutual exchange of effort, loyalty, and value in relationships.
Context : Modern relationships reward women who extract effort without giving back; men must enforce reciprocity or walk away.
Relevance : Reciprocity is a non-negotiable boundary —no free labor, no one-sided investments.


**Relational Attunement**
Definition : The ability to read and respond to relationship dynamics with precision.
Context : Weak men misread signals (e.g., silence = disinterest); strong men decode manipulation and act decisively.
Relevance : Relational attunement is a tactical advantage , not a weakness.

**Resilience**
Definition : The capacity to adapt to adversity through iterative learning and disciplined recovery.
Context : Nice guys break under rejection; alphas treat failure as feedback.
Relevance : Resilience is strategic evolution —using setbacks to refine dominance.

**Simp Cycle**
Definition : A pattern where men give endlessly to women who offer nothing in return.
Context : Simps tolerate disrespect, pay for dates, and suppress their needs to avoid conflict.
Relevance : The book teaches how to exit the simp cycle through boundaries, value creation, and brotherhood .

**Status Instincts**
Definition : The evolved drive to climb dominance hierarchies to secure mating access.
Context : Modern status (wealth, ambition) replaces ancestral dominance (physical strength), but many men still suppress ambition.
Relevance : Men must build status through competence , not compliance, to attract loyalty.

**Strategic Abundance**
Definition : Operating from surplus—multiple connections, skills, and purposes—to avoid dependency.
Context : Scarcity makes men desperate; abundance makes them unreplaceable.
Relevance : Strategic abundance is the ultimate counter to hypergamy , letting men lead rather than beg.

**Tactical Vulnerability**

Definition : Controlled emotional disclosure that builds trust without weakness.
Context : Simps whine about their flaws; alphas frame vulnerability as evidence of growth.
Relevance : Vulnerability isn't a flaw—it's a negotiation tool when used strategically.

## Toxic Masculinity
Definition : A pejorative term used to shame men for dominance, ambition, and risk-taking.
Context : Feminism weaponized the term to neuter male power.
Relevance : The book reframes these traits as weaponized masculinity , essential for dominance.

## Transactional Desperation
Definition : Desperation that drives men to offer endless value without reciprocity.
Context : Transactional desperation fuels the simp cycle, where men trade effort for scraps of approval.
Relevance : Men must replace transactional desperation with value creation —building worth outside romantic contexts.

## Unavailability
Definition : A mindset and strategy where men refuse to beg for attention or tolerate disrespect.
Context : Women pursue men who are emotionally or socially "unavailable," not those who beg for approval.
Relevance : Unavailability is the ultimate weapon —forcing women to invest in you rather than discard you.

## Weaponized Masculinity
Definition : Traditional male traits (dominance, ambition, physical strength) redirected into modern tools for power.
Context : Feminism demonized these traits; the book reframes them as tactical assets .

Relevance : Weaponized masculinity isn't aggression—it's control , clarity , and dominance .

### Alpha Male
Definition : A man who commands respect through confidence, competence, and unapologetic self-respect.
Context : Alpha males dominate evolutionary and modern hierarchies, securing mating access through dominance, not compliance.
Relevance : The book avoids glorifying brute force; instead, it defines alpha behavior as strategic presence .

### Ancestral Algorithms
Definition : Evolutionary instincts that shaped mate selection, parental investment, and dominance hierarchies.
Context : These algorithms still influence modern preferences (e.g., women prioritizing status) despite cultural shifts.
Relevance : Understanding ancestral logic helps men hack the system rather than surrender to it.

### Attachment Blueprints
Definition : Early-life bonding patterns that shape adult relationship behaviors.
Context : Anxious and avoidant styles sabotage modern relationships by creating imbalance.
Relevance : The book teaches how to rewrite insecure blueprints through earned security and brotherhood.

### Bargain (Traditional Male)
Definition : The historical exchange of provision and protection for female loyalty.
Context : Feminism dismantled the provider script but offered no replacement, leaving men adrift.
Relevance : Men must redefine value through competence, dominance, and purpose.

**Conversational Mastery**
Definition : The ability to control interactions through mirroring, calibrated vulnerability, and dominance.
Context : Nice guys lose by apologizing; alphas win by owning the conversation .
Relevance : Conversational dominance is a tactical skill , not an innate trait.

**Digital Intimacy**
Definition : Online interactions that simulate connection but lack real-world reciprocity.
Context : Dating apps and social media create false intimacy, trapping men in transactional cycles.
Relevance : Men must exit the digital bazaar and build real bonds through physical training and skill guilds.

**Dominance Hierarchies**
Definition : Social structures where men earn respect through competence, confidence, and presence.
Context : Evolution built these hierarchies; modern culture vilifies them, leaving men adrift.
Relevance : Men must reclaim dominance hierarchies through brotherhood and skill mastery.

**Earned Security**
Definition : Emotional stability built through deliberate practice, not inherited from childhood.
Context : Anxiously or avoidantly attached men can rewrite their code through presence, competence, and brotherhood.
Relevance : Earned security is armor against vulnerability exploitation .

**Evolutionary Psychology**
Definition : The study of how ancestral survival strategies shape

modern behavior.

Context : Explains female hypergamy, male competition, and mismatch in modern relationships.

Relevance : Provides a scientific foundation for the book's argument that biology is a tool, not a prison.

## Feminism (Second-Wave)

Definition : A movement that dismantled traditional male roles without offering replacement frameworks.

Context : Second-wave feminism destroyed the provider script, leaving men without purpose.

Relevance : The book critiques feminism's war on masculine utility but acknowledges its gains for women.

## Ghosting

Definition : Sudden withdrawal from communication to avoid confrontation.

Context : Women use ghosting to test men's desperation; men use it to enforce boundaries.

Relevance : Silence is a tactical weapon when used intentionally, not reactively.

## Mate Choice Copying

Definition : A strategy where women assess a man's value based on others 'interest (e.g., social proof).

Context : Women prioritize men who are "in demand," ignoring simps who offer free labor.

Relevance : Men must manufacture scarcity to trigger mate choice copying.

## Mate Value

Definition : A person's desirability based on evolved and cultural preferences (e.g., status, ambition, physical presence).

Context : Mate value isn't fixed; it's built through competence, dominance, and unavailability.

Relevance : Men must increase mate value through skill mastery and strategic abundance.

## Resentment Loop
Definition : A cycle of covert contracts, people-pleasing, and entitlement that fuels bitterness.
Context : Simps fall into resentment when their effort goes unrewarded; alphas break the loop through dominance.
Relevance : The book provides scripts to exit the loop and reclaim control.

## Sexual Strategies Theory
Definition : The idea that men and women adopt different mating tactics based on evolutionary pressures.
Context : Women seek providers and genetic upgrades; men compete for mating access through dominance.
Relevance : The book shows how to hack sexual strategies through status, presence, and unavailability.

## Status Signaling
Definition : Behaviors that communicate dominance, competence, or social rank.
Context : Women evolved to notice status; modern men must signal value through skill, posture, and purpose.
Relevance : Status signaling is tactical , not superficial—dominance wins.

## Strategic Abundance
Definition : A mindset where men operate from surplus (multiple connections, skills, purposes) to avoid desperation.
Context : Scarcity makes men disposable; abundance makes them unreplaceable.
Relevance : The book frames abundance as economic warfare against hypergamy.

**Weaponized Vulnerability**
Definition : Disclosing weakness as evidence of growth, not weakness itself.
Context : Simps whine; alphas frame vulnerability as proof of strength .
Relevance : Vulnerability is a negotiation tool , not a surrender.

**Alpha Male**
Definition : A man who commands respect through presence, competence, and unapologetic self-respect.
Context : Historically, alphas secured mating access through dominance; today, they win through confidence and unavailability.
Relevance : The book redefines alpha behavior as tactical dominance , not brute force.

**Ancestral Algorithms**
Definition : Evolutionary instincts that shaped mating, parenting, and status competition.
Context : These algorithms still influence modern attraction, despite cultural shifts.
Relevance : Men must hack ancestral logic , not reject it.

**Attachment Blueprints**
Definition : Early-life bonding patterns that shape adult relationships (secure, anxious, avoidant).
Context : Anxious men chase approval; avoidant men flee conflict. Both styles lead to exploitation.
Relevance : Men must rewrite insecure blueprints through earned security and brotherhood.

**Bargain (Traditional Male)**
Definition : The pre-feminist exchange of provision/protective labor for female loyalty.

Context : Feminism dismantled this bargain, leaving men without purpose.
Relevance : Men must reclaim value through competence, dominance, and purpose.

## Coercion
Definition : The use of force or threats to control others.
Context : Not all coercion is physical—women use emotional coercion to extract effort.
Relevance : Men must avoid coercion but enforce boundaries tactically.

## Competence
Definition : The ability to do hard things, solve problems, and create value.
Context : Evolution rewarded competent men; modern society often punishes them.
Relevance : Competence is the bedrock of self-worth , not compliance.

## Conversational Mastery
Definition : Tactical communication skills that dominate interactions (mirroring, calibrated vulnerability, dominance).
Context : Nice guys beg for approval; alphas control conversations.
Relevance : Conversational dominance is a tactical skill , not a personality trait.

## Digital Intimacy
Definition : Online relationships that simulate closeness but lack real reciprocity.
Context : Dating apps exploit men's need for connection, creating addiction and exploitation.
Relevance : Men must opt out of digital intimacy and build real bonds through brotherhood.

**Dominance Hierarchies**
Definition : Social structures where men earn respect through competence and presence.
Context : Modern culture vilifies dominance, but dominance hierarchies still exist.
Relevance : Men must reclaim dominance through skill mastery and leadership.

**Earned Security**
Definition : Emotional stability built through self-mastery, not inherited from childhood.
Context : Anxiously attached men chase approval; avoidant men withdraw.
Relevance : Earned security is a weapon against vulnerability exploitation.

**Evolutionary Psychology**
Definition : The study of how ancestral survival strategies shape modern behavior.
Context : Explains female hypergamy, male competition, and mismatch in modern relationships.
Relevance : Provides a scientific foundation for the book's argument that biology is a tool, not a prison.

**Feminism (Second-Wave)**
Definition : A movement that dismantled traditional male roles without offering replacement frameworks.
Context : Second-wave feminism destroyed the provider script, leaving men adrift.
Relevance : Men must reclaim utility through competence, dominance, and purpose.

**Gender Roles**
Definition : Cultural scripts defining male and female behavior

(e.g., provision, submission).
Context : Feminism rejected rigid roles but failed to offer men new frameworks.
Relevance : Men must rewrite their roles through weaponized masculinity.

## Gottman's Repair Techniques
Definition : Communication strategies to de-escalate conflict and rebuild trust.
Context : Weak men overuse repair to appease; strong men use it to regain control .
Relevance : The book teaches how to use repair techniques without surrender.

## Hard No
Definition : A refusal that enforces boundaries without apology.
Context : Nice guys justify compliance; alphas use hard nos to demand respect.
Relevance : Hard nos are tactical weapons that filter out users.

## Hypergamy
Definition : The female instinct to seek partners who offer genetic or social upgrades.
Context : Even in egalitarian relationships, women prioritize men who out-earn or out-earn them.
Relevance : Men must compete through dominance , not compliance.

## Integrity
Definition : Adherence to personal values despite external pressure.
Context : Simps abandon integrity to please women; alphas enforce it.
Relevance : Integrity is unshakable self-respect , not moralizing.

**Mate Guarding**
Definition : Behaviors that protect romantic investments (e.g., exclusivity, loyalty tests).
Context : Women historically used mate guarding to secure resources; men now need it to avoid being replaced.
Relevance : Mate guarding is obsolete without strategic abundance—build value, not desperation.

**Neuroplasticity**
Definition : The brain's ability to rewire itself through deliberate practice and environmental modeling.
Context : Men can overwrite anxious or avoidant behaviors through skill training and therapy.
Relevance : Neuroplasticity is the rebel's weapon —rewire weakness into dominance.

**Nonviolent Communication (NVC)**
Definition : A framework for resolving conflict through observation, feeling, need, and request.
Context : Weak men use NVC to apologize; strong men use it to set dominance.
Relevance : NVC is tactical clarity , not submission.

**Omega Male**
Definition : A man who fully disengages from mating markets, often in rejection of rigged systems.
Context : Omegas reject competition but lose leverage; alphas reject exploitation while remaining engaged.
Relevance : The book encourages rebellion, not resignation— omega energy is a trap .

**Parental Investment Theory**
Definition : The idea that the sex investing more in offspring (females) becomes selective.

Context : Feminism granted women financial independence but left men without new scripts.
Relevance : Men must redefine investment through competence, dominance, and purpose.

## People-Pleasing
Definition : Suppressing needs to avoid conflict or earn approval.
Context : Nice guys use people-pleasing to earn loyalty; women exploit it.
Relevance : People-pleasing is submission , not virtue.

## Purpose
Definition : Devotion to a cause larger than personal gain (e.g., mentorship, craftsmanship, brotherhood).
Context : Men without purpose become disposable; men with purpose attract loyalty.
Relevance : Purpose is leverage , not charity.

## Relational Attunement
Definition : The ability to read and shape relationship dynamics with precision.
Context : Weak men misread signals; strong men decode them to enforce boundaries.
Relevance : Relational attunement is tactical insight , not passivity.

## Resilience
Definition : The capacity to adapt to adversity through iterative learning and disciplined recovery.
Context : Nice guys break under rejection; alphas use setbacks to refine dominance.
Relevance : Resilience is strategic evolution , not endurance.

## Social Modeling
Definition : The process by which men learn behavior from

peers, mentors, and cultural cues.
Context : Weak men model simps; strong men model warriors, leaders, and craftsmen.
Relevance : Social modeling is tactical evolution —choose your tribe carefully.

## Strategic Abundance
Definition : Operating from surplus (multiple connections, skills, purposes) to avoid desperation.
Context : Scarcity makes men disposable; abundance makes them unreplaceable.
Relevance : Strategic abundance is economic warfare against hypergamy.

## Tactical Vulnerability
Definition : Controlled emotional disclosure that builds trust without weakness.
Context : Nice guys whine; alphas frame vulnerability as evidence of strength.
Relevance : Tactical vulnerability is negotiation , not confession.

## Value Creation
Definition : Building competence, dominance, and purpose to attract loyalty without desperation.
Context : Simps trade effort for approval; alphas trade value for respect.
Relevance : Value creation is economic leverage —stop giving, start trading.

## Weaponized Masculinity
Definition : Traditional male traits (dominance, ambition, physicality) redirected into modern tools for power.
Context : Feminism demonized these traits; the book reframes them as tactical assets .
Relevance : Weaponized masculinity is control , not cruelty.

**Why It Works**

Definition : A framework for evaluating actions based on results, not intentions.

Context : Nice guys fail because their effort isn't rewarded; alphas win because their dominance is.

Relevance : "Why it works" is tactical clarity —measure success, not intent.

**Yield**

Definition : Surrendering effort without return—e.g., paying for dates with no loyalty.

Context : Simps yield endlessly; alphas demand reciprocity.

Relevance : Yield is submission , not generosity.

**Zero-Sum Game**

Definition : A system where one person's gain equals another's loss (e.g., dating apps, career hierarchies).

Context : Modern relationships are zero-sum; men must dominate, not negotiate.

Relevance : The book rejects zero-sum thinking by teaching men to create value, not compete for scraps.

Made in the USA
Monee, IL
31 May 2025